THE
PRESIDENT'S
SECRET
IMs

THE
PRESIDENT'S
SECRET
IMs

DANIELLE CRITTENDEN

SSE

SIMON SPOTLIGHT ENTERTAINMENT

NEW YORK   LONDON   TORONTO   SYDNEY

SSE

SIMON SPOTLIGHT ENTERTAINMENT
An imprint of Simon & Schuster
1230 Avenue of the Americas, New York, New York 10020
SIMON SPOTLIGHT ENTERTAINMENT and related logo are
trademarks of Simon & Schuster, Inc.
Design by Jane Archer and Margaret Gallagher
Emoticon illustrations by Jane Archer
Manufactured in the United States of America
First Edition 10 9 8 7 6 5 4 3 2 1
Library of Congress Cataloging-in-Publication Data
Crittenden, Danielle, 1963–
The president's secret IMs / Danielle Crittenden.–1st ed.
p. cm.
ISBN-13: 978-1-4169-4749-3
ISBN-10: 1-4169-4749-3
[1. Bush, George W. (George Walker), 1946–Humor. 2. United States–Politics and
government–2001–Humor. 3. Presidents–United States–Humor. 4. Instant messaging–
United States–Humor.] I. Title. II. Title: President's secret instant messages.
E903.3.C75   2007
973.93102'07–dc22
2007007763

This book is dedicated to:

loveMANDS
Miranda Frum

yankeeguy
Nathaniel Frum

PrincessRanger
Beatrice Frum

WAHOO! NEWS

White House in turmoil following leak of president's personal IM conversations

AP - **22 minutes ago**

WASHINGTON—The White House is scrambling to offset "inestimable" political damage caused by the leak of President Bush's personal instant message conversations. Transcripts of the online chats reveal a shockingly candid, profane president who refers to America's terrorist enemies as "Islamonuts," among other embarrassing revelations.

White House spokesman Tony Snow has called a press conference at 12 p.m. EDT to explain how the president's private "iChats" were obtained by a blogger at the online journal Huffingtonpost.com and published in paperback today by Simon Spotlight Entertainment.

The rambling, inflammatory, and at times incoherent conversations, conducted under the screen name "Kickass43," date back to the beginning of Bush's second term. The president's "Buddy List" represents a Who's Who of top political staff and world leaders, ranging from Karl Rove and Condoleezza Rice to Bill Clinton, Tony Blair, and even the Pope.

RELATED COVERAGE

•Hillary Clinton insists marriage "still strong" despite secret plot hatched by husband Bill, President Bush to sink her political campaign, as revealed by IMs (AP—1 hour, 11 minutes ago)

•Six suicide bombers, beloved American icon Mr. Peanut dead after Muslims protest president's "Islamonut" comment (AP—36 minutes ago)

•Disgraced congressman Mark Foley calls for president's resignation (AP—17 minutes ago)

•Online glossary for IM language

•Click here to see the president's "Buddy List"

Home > News & Policies > Press Secretary Briefings

Press Briefing by Tony Snow

White House Conference Center Briefing Room 12:04 P.M. EDT

MR. SNOW: Welcome to the White House briefing with Tony Snow. I'm Tony Snow. We'll be getting to today's big story in just a moment. Quickly, let me just run through the president's schedule for the remainder of the day. At three p.m. there will be an elm tree planting on the north grounds. Then the president will meet with National Merit Scholars. After that he has a phone call scheduled with the prime minister of Bermuda on issues relating to the preservation of endangered reefs.

Thus we don't have a lot of time to take all the questions about what some of you are now calling "iGate." Let me just

say that the president regards this as an outrageous leak and extreme violation of his privacy, one that has put the nation's security gravely at risk. We are attempting to get to the bottom of this leak. An internal investigation has been launched. We would not rule out the possibility of partisanship playing a role in this, but beyond that I'm not going to say more until we have concluded our internal investigation. As for the actual content of the online chats, I would say there's no story here. It's old news. The president, like anyone else, lets off steam and tells jokes in his personal communications. If there's any news, it's that the president's a lot smarter and funnier than you guys give him credit for. Okay, let's go to your questions. Why don't I bite the bullet and start with David Gregory? He looks like he's ready to jump out of his chair.

Q Frankly, I'm astonished that your talking point of the day is that there's "no story here." This story is rocking the entire nation. Just for starters, we've discovered that the president had been plotting with former President Clinton to defeat Hillary Clinton's presidential campaign—

MR. SNOW: That was all in good fun, David. In fact, Senator Clinton and the president shared a hearty laugh about it this morning when he called her—

Q I'm not finished. He speculated about nuking Iran and North Korea—

MR. SNOW: Hey, haven't we all? As I said, you have to read these conversations in the context of a joke. J-O-K-E—

Q He refers to our Arab allies as "Islamonuts." How is that a joke?

MR. SNOW: With all due respect, Helen, your reputation has not been not built on your sense of humor. Let's go to *La Presse*.

Q The president of France has issued a statement suggesting that he will no longer cooperate with your foreign policy because of the president's ridicule of the French people—

Q Signor Snow, on behalf of the Italian media I must ask you to explain your president's request that our former prime minister, how you say, "take out" some critics—

Q You haven't responded to my question about nuking.

MR. SNOW: Whoa, whoa. I can't answer questions if you all speak at once. David, I believe I already answered your question. Now let's go to CNN.

Q Let me pick up on nuking Iran and North Korea. Was this really a "joke"? And if so, would you say it's appropriate for the president to make these jokes at a truly sensitive moment in diplomatic negotiations?

MR. SNOW: Beyond saying, as I've already said, that the president was engaging in light humor, I'm going to dodge that question and tell you why I'm dodging it. It would jeopardize our nation's security to say more at this time.

Q Don't you think the president has already seriously jeopardized the nation's security?

Q I'd like to move the topic to the president's sexist characterization of Condoleezza Rice and other female officials as "hot."

Q Has the First Lady issued any statement on his resentment about buying her an anniversary present?

Q What about his solution to the Palestinian problem as razing the Authority's territory and building condos in its place?

MR.SNOW: As I feared, we're out of time. But let me just end by saying that we are investigating the leak, and when I have more information on that I will let you know. The president is dismayed and disappointed over this egregious violation of his privacy. Given how concerned many of you have been about these privacy issues in general, he knows you will understand how important it is that innocent citizens such as himself should not be subject to this kind of blatant breach of personal security. Indeed, he has worked tirelessly to ensure that only those suspected of terrorism would be subject to this kind of scrutiny. With that, ladies and gentlemen, we have an elm to plant.

END 12:17 EDT

The
President's
SECRET
IMs

the President's Buddy List

(in alphabetical order)

Ben16
Pope Benedict XVI

BigBartlett
Dan Bartlett, Counselor to the President

BigEar
General Michael Hayden, head of the CIA

BigMacher
Ariel Sharon

ChiefScooty
Scooter Libby, former Chief of Staff to Dick Cheney

FlyChopper
Josh Bolten, Chief of Staff

GinRummy
Donald Rumsfeld

Hillary08
Hillary Clinton

HMiers
Harriet Miers, former WH counsel and
nominee to Supreme Court

Hot_Librarian
First Lady Laura Bush

IheartUSA
Karen Hughes, former Counselor to the President;
now Undersecretary, Public Diplomacy

Ladeezman42
Bill Clinton

LeGrandFromage
Jacques Chirac, President of France

Nap0leon3
Silvio Berlusconi, former Prime Minister of Italy

NationalSecurityGuy
Stephen Hadley, National Security Advisor

Party_gurl
Jenna Bush

SecretAgentMan
Porter Goss, former CIA director

SecStateUSA
Condoleezza Rice

SheikMo
The Sheikh of Dubai

Snoblowr
Tony Snow, Press Secretary

Str8talk08
John McCain

SumNobel4u2
Bono

Supremegrrl
Harriet Miers, former WH counsel and
nominee to Supreme Court

Sxybritguy10
Tony Blair

TheWizOoz
John Howard, Prime Minister of Australia

Ugogrl
Nancy Pelosi

Veepman
Dick Cheney

Wonderboy
Karl Rove

○○○   chat with Ladeezman42

10:07 p.m.

yo bill

u up?

man im always up

whazzup witu

aint it past ur bedtime 😊

laura kickd me out

bin ther dude

sed my tossin n turnin keepin her up

in my case thers uslly a flyin lamp involvd

LOL

y don't u go down 2 the alley

bowl a few frames

order in sum domino's

thats wat i did wen nuffin else wuz goin on

man i miss that

chat with Ladeezman42

dont like bowlin alone

used 2 bowl w harriet

shes not talkin 2 me

evr sins i sed i made a mistake

bin THER dude

dont kno wat 2 do

man she mus b sum hot chick

harriet??

rofl

how else a chick like that get SCOTUS?

wat she do 2 u??

its always the *quiet* 1s

the quote unquote librarians

theyr WILDCATS

its not like that dude

the closet in the map room rite?

man i can C it

its NOT. LIKE. THAT.

K???

k

sry

but it had 2 b sumpin like that rite?

its SCOTUS man

evn my hottest chicks only got state jobs

xept monica

she got an ol poetry book of hillarys

sum cheapshit bling & like a tshirt

wuz nuffin like that

nuffin i sed

nuffin?

???

🙄

u nuts man!

u mus b smokin sum crazy stuff

i'll b honest

my old man sed u & i shd talk

ask u wat 2 do

ur old man rox

luv that guy

i kno

ur like best buds now

he dont want 2 golf w me no mor

hes like hangin w the cool kids

katrina wuz awsum

u shoulda seen it dude

i DID c it

o yeh

4got

so wat do i do?

need ur help man

im in BIG trble

thatsa joke—u & me im-ing

wat if the dems get whiff of it??

not gd 4 me eithr

yeh but im like a hero now

im the frikkin gd ol days

1st time in my life i got moola

its falling outta my freakin pockets

all these speeches

(btw thanx 4 the tax cut!)

so if u screw up we r all toast

not 2 mention hillary mite actlly WIN

i aint no 1st gent if u kno wat im sayin

fine i'll help

jus dont tell any1

k??

k

thanx

k so wat ur posse tellin u 2 do?

theyr like all bout 2 b indicted

& the girlfriends aint speakin 2 me

theyr like hangin in the bathroom w harriet

im havin majr dejavu

wish harriet wd just say thanx but no thanx u kno 😞

once u give these chix sumpin u cant nvr ask 4 it back

they wont give it 2 u

man they wont evn dryclean it!

my base is fumin

im like *trust me*

it aint workin

im sry but thats soooo lame

they aint gna trust u

no 1 evr trustd ME

but i did wat i liked

u evr hear me ask 4 trust??

no

ive had nuff lamps thrown at my hed k

k

NVR say *trust me*

thats ur 1st problem

numero 2:

u guys r fightin like a buncha hall monitors

gotta knock the shit outta ur critics

srsly u gotta hit hard

like how?

dirty shit man

remember that kathleen willey chix cat?

uh no

1 of them chix who sed i came on 2 her . . . ?

kinda lost count . . .

no mattr

my pt: that chix cat had a lttl *accident*

cats w skidmarx send the msg dude

as 4 harriet . . . howz her *health* 🙂

!!

8

😮

cant go ther man!!

yes u can

get creative

duz NIH got sum advans copies of that bird flu?

wd nvr DO that!!!

not u frat boy

1 of ur buds

i dont have buds like that!

how u guys won 04 beats the crap outta me

i jus need harriet 2 step down

dont need 2 frikkin *off* her

shes a sweet lttl lady

heck she duz meals on wheels

if u dont take care of it i'll haf 2 ok?

cuz this is real bad 4 me

ttlly sux

o man—Hills tryin 2 IM me!

just gotta msg!

c wat im sayin dude?!!!!

u gotta fix this!!

ill c wat i can do

but no1s gonna hurt harriet—or her cat

fine do it ur way

u can always come up w a scandal

mayb shes a secret boozr & gamblr

holyrollers hate that shit

remember john tower?

k k

jus leave it 2 me

10

11:01 p.m.

Are you still up?

jus goin 2 bed hon

What are you up to?

nuffin

Truthfully?

u huh

srsly

u gotta trust me on this 1 babe . . .

chat with Sxybritguy10

8:29 p.m.

hey

Auto-reply: The prime minister of the United Kingdom of Great Britain and Northern Ireland is offline.

yo tony

u ther??

o man

im sooo bord

chat with SecStateUSA

8:33 p.m.

I see you're online, Mr. President.

hey condi!!

dat u grrrl?? ☺

Yes, sir. I wondered if there was anything outstanding to discuss before I left the office.

how u doin GF?

how u DOIN homegirl?

Please, Mr. President.

sry

keep forgettin u dont do the * blak * thing

No, sir.

colin didnt mind

he did a wickd jesse jackson

So you've told me, sir.

rite

ur rents did the marchin so u dont have 2 do the blak thing yadda yadda

Yes, sir. They are big sticklers for proper grammar.

uh huh

They made great economic sacrifices in order to pay for my concert piano lessons

got it

and sent me to college at a time when African-American women . . .

K!!!

Thank you, sir.

Well, now that summer's over it's "back to school" for us, as it were, isn't it, Mr. President? Time to get back to the old DC campus. Back to the heavy lifting.

wuz nvr gd @ that

at skool anyway 😊

bin doin alotta heavy liftin down in crawford tho

Yes. I'm sorry about that, Mr. President. Wasn't much of a vacation for you this year, was it, sir? All that Cindy Sheehan business.

i meant the brush

had 2 keep liftin the frikkin stuff 4 the fotogs

give em sumpin else 2 take fotos of other than those dam protesters

nrly put my back out!

then there wuz that bike ride w lance armstrong 😳

I thought you did well, sir.

LOL!! fittest prez in histry & couldn't keep up w a dam cancer patient!!

He is a world champion, sir.

the whole trip wuz a ttl bummr

couldnt leave the ranch w/out michael moore wannabes in my face

put a crimp in bowlin nite

The press was just bored, Mr. President.

It makes me think you should consider vacationing elsewhere next year.

??

☹

Seriously. If you recall, President Reagan got great press in Santa Barbara—and he took as many weeks off, not to mention naps, as you do, sir.

If I remember correctly, the daily press briefing was scheduled to give the press enough time to get down to Los Angeles afterward for dinner.

no way u r gettin me 2 the left coast

i'll have barbra streisand @ my freakin door

shes wors than cindy

I don't think you have to go to California, sir, but perhaps Karl could book you a place in Hawaii next summer. Or maybe Martha's Vineyard. The press loves Martha's Vineyard.

aint fleein the ranch cuzza bad pre

u kno me 2 well 4 that

dont flee nowher cuzza bad press

gotta complete the mission of my vacation

Just a suggestion, sir. You could always pop down there for weekends.

sry GF—aint a wuss

speakin of wusses u see tony took his vacation @ an "undisclosed location"

I did, sir. In fact I visited him "there" and we did some great Jet-Skiing.

veep's always doin that

Jet-Skiing?!

rofl

i mean goin fly fishin & stuff in "undisclosed locations"

like its sum security thing

basically he duznt want war crazies plantin crosses outside his tent

Are those down yet?

no

the secret service is waitin 4 the press 2 leave b4 they raze em

cn hardly wait

its lookin like arlington cemetery out ther

You'll forget it all once you're back in Washington.

nvr thot id want 2 get bak 2 that swamp so quik

only fun wuz when u came down

I always enjoy myself in Crawford, sir.

xept 4 the grub

You're an excellent cook, Mr. President.

cmon—y u not like my bbq?

u folks supposd 2 like bbq

Please, sir. Just because I'm African-American . . .

rite rite sry

im wite & i LUV bbq

its not a race thing

If you really wish to know why I didn't like that PARTICULAR barbecued chicken, Mr. President, it was because of the sauce. I'm not partial to that sauce.

?!

its my moms recipe!!

u mix mayo w kraft french dressin

brown sugar

sum catsup (not heinz!!)

Exactly. No offense to your mother, sir—who is always a hoot, by the way, and she looked fabulous—but that sauce is what the neo-cons would describe as "goyish."

so shoot me im a goy

& no offense c-grl but now ur soundin blak

dont like * wite * bbq sauce

It's hardly "black," Mr. President, to prefer Tex-Mex. Next time I'll bring you a recipe from Bobby Flay.

speakin of goys how goes gaza?

Strictly speaking, sir, Palestinians aren't traditionaly referred to as "goys" by the Jewish people.

duh

theyr shvarzes

That's a very derogatory term, Mr. President.

rlly?

i thot it wuz hebrew 4 arab

Yiddish, sir. But it doesn't mean "Arab." In any case, I think the pull-out went well. Restarting the peace talks will of course be a lengthy process . . .

wat duz it mean?

Had a good phone call last night with Mahmoud

cmon

pls tell me

and he's optimistic about Gaza's future.

o rite

hes ttlly welcome 2 that ttlly shit piece of real estate

isrealis r smart. u gotta give em that

Of course, sir.

if thers 1 thing they kno its real estate

like y keep that piece of shit?

they spent $$$$ 2 defend it

& 4 wat?

8000 freakin loser settlrs

man it wouldve been cheapr 2 buy em all condos on the upr west side

I agree, Mr. President. But despite the Palestinian Authority's optimism, if the Israelis don't keep order there anymore, the job will fall to us.

so wat else is nu

Unless our European allies agree to help out.

o sure

Right. So Gaza will be our problem now.

like thanx. like we dont have enuff on r plate w iraq

Or Iran.

oooo thanx 4 remindin me

Or North Korea.

man ur bummin me out

Sorry, sir.

like i wuznt alredy bummd out

Maybe we should end this session, sir.

Besides, I need to work out before going home.

watu talkin bout?

ur da bod!

ur da sexiest of state!!!

Thank you, Mr. President, but we all can't be as fit as you.

1 last thing b4 u go

Yes, sir?

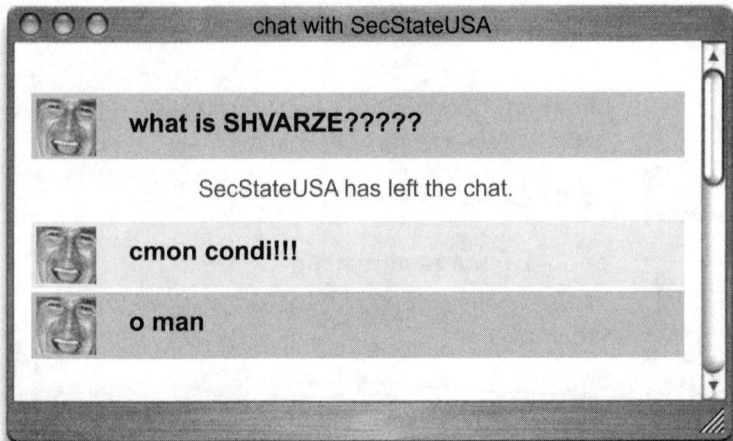

chat with SecStateUSA

what is SHVARZE?????

SecStateUSA has left the chat.

cmon condi!!!

o man

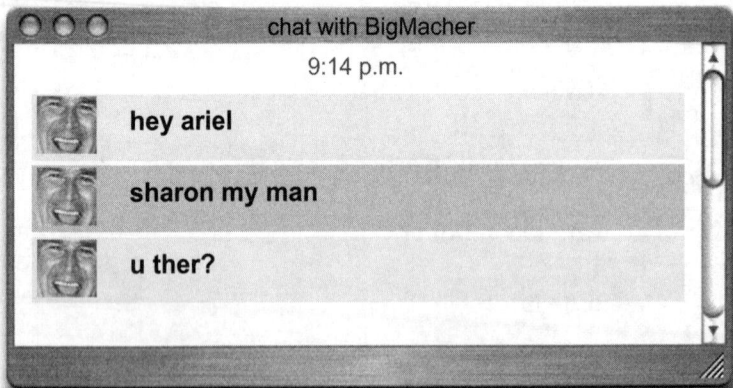

chat with BigMacher

9:14 p.m.

hey ariel

sharon my man

u ther?

3

chat with IheartUSA

7:04 p.m.

Mr. President?

Hello?

yo karen!

gr8 2 hear from u!

how goes the intl tour?

I'm back in Texas, sir.

I think we've managed to make real inroads in Muslim opinion.

Especially with women and children.

I felt they responded well to our message of tolerance and compassion.

And they believe in freedom.

im off 2 kick booty in China!

Read a little texas law 2 em . . .

Ha ha, sir.

I know you'll bring the same message of hope and democracy on your trip through Asia and continue to raise the world's opinion of America.

not so gd @ raisin opinions rite now

thatll change wen votrs c me in mongolia

LUV mongols

tuff ass ppl

bilt a democracy outta nada

sent troops 2 iraq

they scare the shit outta iraqis

last time the mongols hit baghdad

they built a mtn of skulls

mayb we shd do the same

stop listenin 2 all the dems whinin of "lies"

redeclare war

& do the job rite

Yes, sir.

I know you are at your very best when you feel strongly.

24

Our allies may not be ready yet for that level of strength.

What does Karl say?

lol

karls puttin his resume on monster.com

or he bttr b

wonderboy let me down big time w *plamegate*

got him runnin round shorin up the base

So it's good I'm back, sir.

darn rite

And let me say, we need to get you back as well . . .

?

To that man I knew long ago in Dallas . . .

To the man who stared personal disaster in the face . . .

who rose to become president of the United States.

okaaay

He didn't rise by isolating himself.

He rose by looking deep into himself . . .

Seeing the man he could be . . .

And with the help of the Lord, lifting himself up from despair . . .

to lead a nation under siege.

that man didn't hav pollstrs

39%!!

😮

Yes, well, that's not as good as it could be.

I've been thinking a lot about it.

And I have some suggestions.

?

First, sir, with all due respect, you're too angry.

You LOOK angry..

Every time I see you on television you're acting like Barney just peed on the rug.

lol

Seriously, sir.

You're wagging your finger and shaking your head.

I worry you're about to roll up the newspaper

and smack the electorate on the nose.

k

will wrk on that

what else?

Australia.

wat about it?

I notice it's not on the schedule of your Asian tour.

duh

thats cuz its not in Asia

I realize that, sir. But it's not far.

You could pop down.

Shore up your image with a loyal and important ally.

John Howard is extremely popular.

I see a good photo op.

Both of you in blue shirts and those "Crocodile Dundee" hats.

Could bring us back some security moms.

ur getting rusty GF

danny boy alredy checkd it out

johno duznt want 2 be seen w me rite now

like my bud tony

things r bettr 4 em if we dont look 2 close

npda

Excuse me?

I don't do this IM thing often, sir.

no public displays of affection

Okay, sir.

Then I have a backup plan.

Send ME to Australia

send U?

2 oz?

☺

Yes, sir.

They experienced a very close brush with terrorism.

The people of Australia are worried and concerned.

It's a perfect moment for our administration to reach out.

Show compassion.

Show we stand by them.

Show U stand by em

As you said, sir: npda.

I think I've proven that I can represent the United States more than adequately.

I've won the hearts and minds of women all over the Middle East.

It's amazing what just a small display of caring can accomplish.

Picture your special envoy embracing the children of Muslim immigrants in the suburbs of Sydney.

Showing that a safe society doesn't mean an intolerant one.

they cd use sum of ur carin in the paris burbs

thos kids of immigrnts r torchin cars

That's what I mean, sir.

You're angry.

I understand.

But it's time to let go of the anger.

Heal our friends in Australia.

I could go over Christmas.

Take my family.

Besides, the Caribbean is all booked.

y don't we run it by johno

Who, sir?

30

howard

the preem

Terrific. I'll contact the people at State.

no!

wat time is it ovr ther?

In Australia?

It's around lunchtime, I believe.

gd

he'll be online

Do you think it would be better to go through the usual channels, sir?

I'd hate to bother him when he's busy…

heck no

31

7:33 p.m.

wassup johno

gday Georgie!

bad timin?

good timin! just finished shaking hands with the unemployed

Your dedication is impressive, Mr. Prime Minister.

that's strine 4 takin a leak

howz it goin down undr

busy as hell

been goin flat out like a lizard drinkin

roundin up reffos

Who, sir?

u kno

ragheads

your islamic froot loops

we're not poofs like those frogs

wot can I do 4 u 2day Georgie?

we're online w my bud karen

she's a *good sheila*

wants 2 kno if she can visit u @ xmas

that's bonzer

ur a texan rite karen?

Yes, sir.

well then we'll tayk u out 2 the station

shoot sum roos

it'll be a real corker!

Actually, sir, I was hoping for a more official kind of visit.

Your country nearly came under attack.

But thanks to the hard work of your intelligence services

and your first responders

a major disaster was averted.

As a representative of the American people

I'd like to express our solidarity with you and your nation

and our gratitude for your dedication, perseverance, and courage

at the front lines of the War on Terror.

pardon me, karen

dya mind if we hava word in private georgie?

k

scuse us karen

cd u log off 4 a sec?

Yes, sir. Of course.

IheartUSA has left the chat.

wots she yabberin on about???

sry johno

she jus sprung it on me

strewth!

34

the public will have a blue

cant have some wowzer coming over

treatin us like a bunch a whingers

it'll be as useful as lips on a chicken

dont mean to grizzle

ur a good mate

but I reckon I'll spit the dummy if she comes

??

strine 4 "NO"

got it

I'll tell her

there's a good bloke

when they've stopped rubbishin the war

u & I'll have a real ripper

till then we have 2 watch r tipple

35

if u kno wot I mean

4 sur

hang in ther bud

hooroo

TheWizOoz has left the chat.

IheartUSA has joined the chat.

7:48 p.m.

So may I go, sir?

duznt look gd big K

he sez the timin is a littl bit dicky

"Dicky," sir?

strine for not gd

Really, sir, I think I could make a difference . . .

come 2 camp dave 4 xmas instead

dont hav no roos

we can alwys make the secret service dudes dance

36

I'm rolling on the floor laughing, sir.

ur gettin it

**not bad 4 a conch who
duznt kno xmas from bourke st**

sir??

jus sumpin i pickd up from johno

Bon voyage, Mr. President.

puhleez

no french!

4

chat with Veepman

9:46 p.m.

yo dick

Auto-reply: The vice president of the United States is in an undisclosed location.

chat with SecStateUSA

9:47 p.m.

hey condi wassup

u ther GF?

Auto-reply: Secretary Rice is currently out of the country. For general inquiries, please contact the State Department at www.state.gov. If you wish to schedule a media interview, award an honorary doctorate, or book Dr. Rice for your next event, please contact the secretary's office. On the main directory, press options #, 3, and 5, and then follow the directions.

chat with Wonderboy

9:48 p.m.

karl

hel-LO

they aint got nuffin on u!

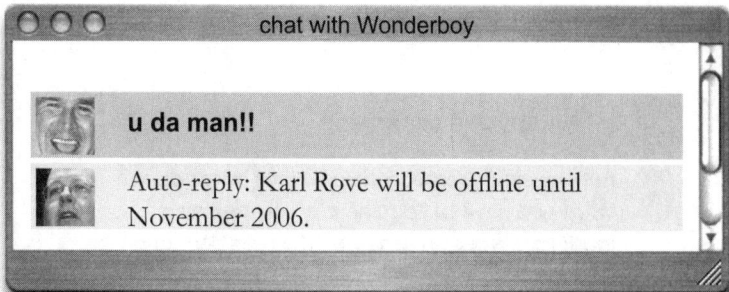

chat with Wonderboy

u da man!!

Auto-reply: Karl Rove will be offline until November 2006.

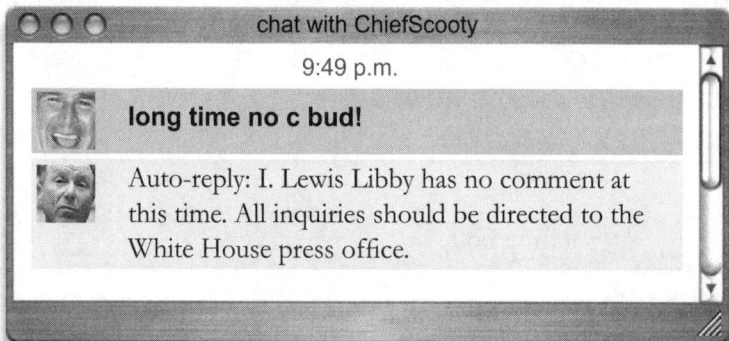

chat with ChiefScooty

9:49 p.m.

long time no c bud!

Auto-reply: I. Lewis Libby has no comment at this time. All inquiries should be directed to the White House press office.

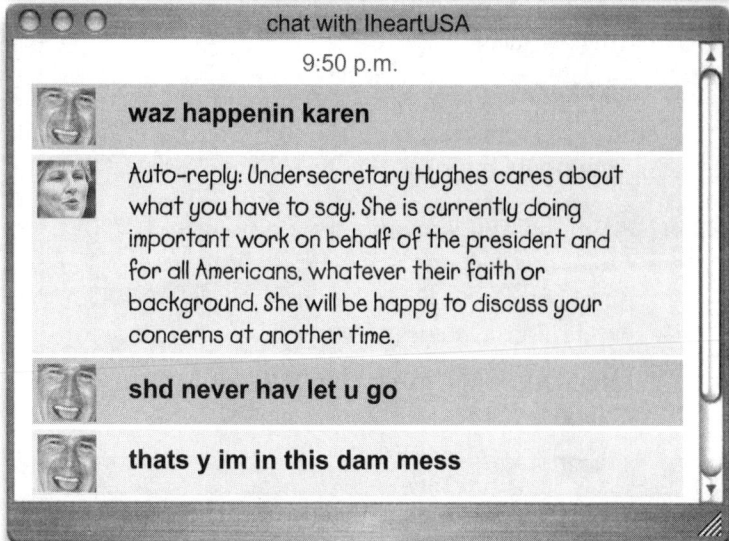

chat with IheartUSA

9:50 p.m.

waz happenin karen

Auto-reply: Undersecretary Hughes cares about what you have to say. She is currently doing important work on behalf of the president and for all Americans, whatever their faith or background. She will be happy to discuss your concerns at another time.

shd never hav let u go

thats y im in this dam mess

chat with IheartUSA

u kept my sry ass in line

Auto-reply: Undersecretary Hughes cares about what you have to say. She is currently doing important work on behalf of the president and for all Americans, whatever their faith or background. She will be happy to discuss your concerns at another time.

chat with BigBartlett

9:52 p.m.

yo danny boy

Auto-reply: It is important for conservatives to reserve judgment, give the candidate a chance to prove herself at the hearings, and trust the president.

???

danno its me 😊

Auto-reply: It is important for conservatives to reserve judgment, give the candidate a chance to prove herself at the hearings, and trust the president.

thats ur frikkin away msg????

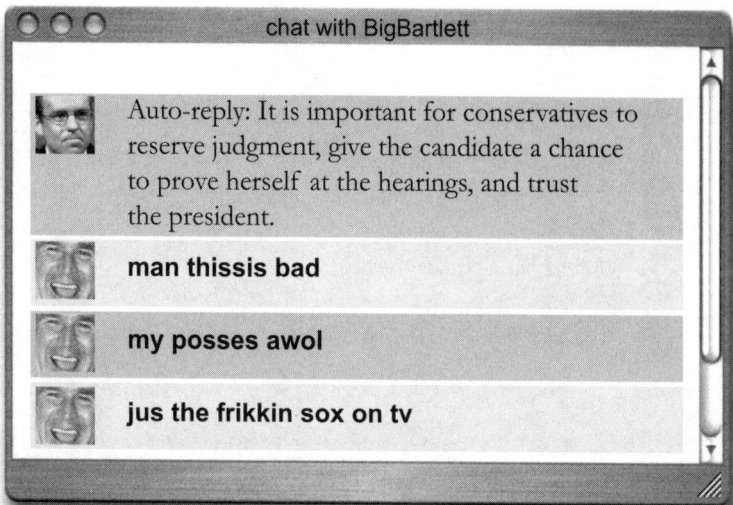

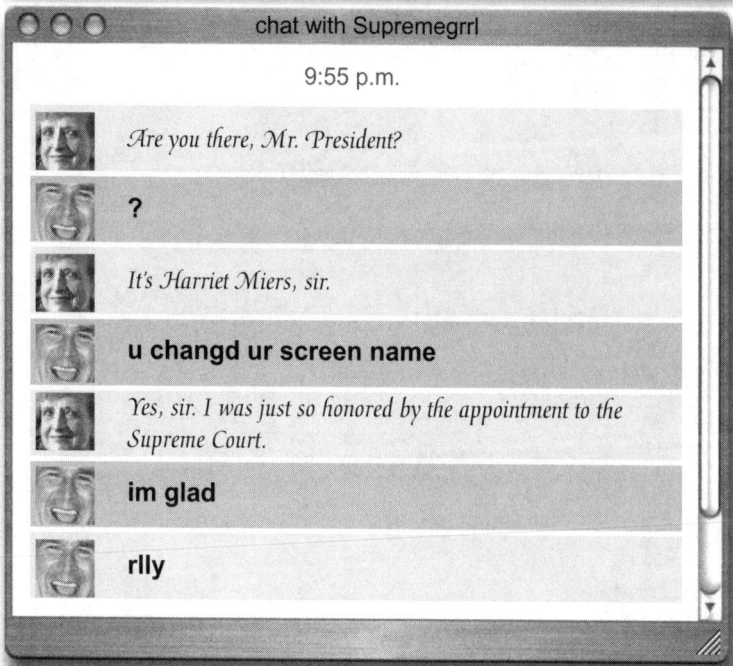

I know it's been tough on you these past weeks

All the criticism we've endured from the right AND left

But we knew that was coming.

We knew it wasn't going to be easy.

sure

And you've so loyally stood by me.

I really can't thank you enough.

rite

There aren't a lot of men like you out there.

If there were I might have married one of them. 😉

mayb we shd talk

Certainly, sir.

bout this SCOTUS bizness

That's a great idea.

I've got some ideas for our strategy going forward.

The First Lady had some terrific suggestions as well.

u spoke w numero uno???

She's been very helpful. And as always, a dear friend.

. . .

. . .

(this is sooooo hard 4 me 2 say!)

What is it, sir?

thers bin a teeny tiny mistake

A mistake?

yeh

Is it something I can correct, sir?

o yeh

What is it, Mr. President?

Tell me so I can help!

Are you still there?

How bad a mistake is it?

Worse than letting WMDs into the 2003 State of the Union?

You know I still regret that very, very much.

I take full blame for that, sir..

I can't understand why my Wite-Out pen didn't catch it. 🙁

almost as bad as that

Please tell me!

You know I stand ready to do anything for you.

Remember that time you were running for governor . . .

and you had that inconvenient driving record, as we put it?

k k

this is way different

like TTLLY different

bout that SCOTUS appt . . .

What about it?

44

I made a mistake

a BIG mistake

a big FRIKKIN mistake

there i sed it

Oh.

I understand.

You want me to withdraw my nomination.

NO!!!

You don't?

☺

wat im sayin is . . .

wen i nominatd u 2 *SCOTUS* i made a mistake

dont hav gd speeechriters no mor

& a rlly rlly bad typo crept in

a big fat typo . . .

45

?!

i wuz sposed 2 b nominatin u 2 the IRAQI supreme court

SCOTIQ

they need u ther girl

rlly rlly bad

theyr gna hav a nu constitution like rite away & there aint no top ppl on the court

ur the best we got like I sed

told every1 that

gna make u CHIEF justis of iraq

no mor of these dumbass hearins

so watu think?

u like that?

harriet?

yo harriet

u ther?

Auto-reply: Harriet Miers, Counsel to the President, will be away from her desk this week. Fresh flowers may be delivered c/o the White House staff secretary, who will ensure she receives them. Ms. Miers thanks you for your kind support.

8:26 p.m.

yo prez

?

bono

ur nu *best bud*

sonny?!

i thot u wer ded!!!!

BONO

as in U2

not as in "& cher"

o

u freakd me out

thot i wuz getting msgs from the byond

u kno like hillary & elenor

😮

u goppers r so lame

ur musical knwledj stops at like 1975

not tru

tru

evry time I meet 1 of u dudes u call me BONE-O

like he wuz the original

& im sum knockoff

he wuz a fly dude in congress wat can i say

gop dudes in congress uslly look like mormon choir boyz

bono wuz 2 cool

hot wife b4 she went brunette

big mistake

she duznt look any smarter

jus less hot

rite

change of topic

49

so waddya think of my idea

wat idea

!

my wrld tour 4 hunger

?

man we TALKD bout this

in the OVAL OFFICE.

"ambassador 2 end world poverty"

kickoff concert on the south lawn

ring any bells?

O MAN

you remember!

sox jus scord anudder freakin run

sox sux! sox sux!

ur watching baseball?!

50

duh

its like the WRLD SERIES

astros screwin up big time

like NONE of my teams r workin it

mayb we shd trade rove 4 lidge

(not like hes pitchin any bttr)

I'm sry if I care more bout WORLD HUNGER at the mo

o rite

like if it wuz soccer u wdnt care

xcuse me

football

kidz cud starv if beckham wuz playin

k fine

so waddya think of my idea?

lemme b frank witu:

not 2 good

u likd it at lunch!

yeh but

but wat

gotta lotta ambassdrs rite now

they aint doin so hot

karens doin her evita tour thru islam

like we shda shut that 1 down b4 bringin it 2 broadway

no offnse but wat idiot thought sendin a white evangelical chick from tx . . .

2 preach 2 the jihadists . . .

wuz gonna fly??

guilty

o

sry

no ur rite

but ther aint no persuadin karen

shes like "i kno muslims"

"theyr jus soccr moms w suicide vests"

"leave it 2 me" she sed

i think she was tryin 2 flee the crib b4 the indictments went down

condis way better but 2 b honest shes still not goin ovr

ive played tuff crowds but nothing like arabs

theyr wors than baptists!

condi wuz my mistake 2

thot that part of the wrld wd like a way hot blak chick in big boots kickin ther butt

saudis r kinky that way

think u need 2 send a guy

a brother

jeb?!

lol

an ARAB brother

not 1 of yr good ol boyz with a spray-on tan

wat bout u?

me?

do arabs??

😮

rofl

no doofus brain

im talkin bout africans

dont u hav same problemo as karen & condi?

I dont get wat ur sayin

ur a wite ass

jus becuz u wear those phat suits & wrap glasses

dont make u any less of a wite ass

put a do-rag on ur hed

ur still jus a wite raghed

wat makes u think u can hang w africans any bttr than karen w the durka durkas?

r u dissin me bro?

ive been workin my ass off 4 the africans way long dude

way way longer than geldof

aint gotta nitehood

cuz im a mick

but ive been nominated 4 THE prize

the NOBEL prize

aint dissin u

jus sayin the ambassador thang aint gna b happenin

lemme talk 2 my bud tony

mayb he'll work sumpin 4 u

k

thanx

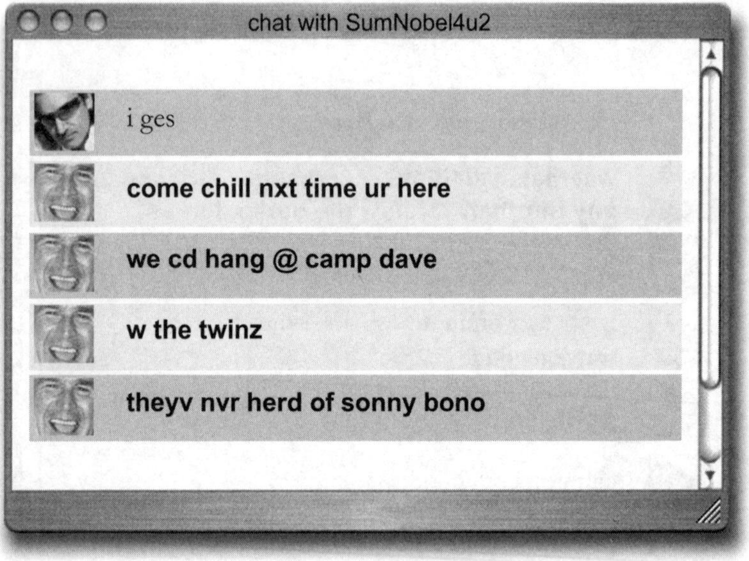
chat with SumNobel4u2
i ges
come chill nxt time ur here
we cd hang @ camp dave
w the twinz
theyv nvr herd of sonny bono

6

chat with Ladeezman42

6:47 p.m.

im on

u ther?

Auto-reply: The president of the United States is not currently online. He is out working hard for the American people.

yo homie

Auto-reply: The president of the United States is not currently online. He is out working hard for the American people.

aw man

cmon

ive gotta date

hey

sry 2 b l8

missus wuz raggin me

4 wat

SCOTUS

sez i shda nominatd anudder chick

sez we hav enuff pasta eaters alredy

she & harriet r like boo hoo

setbak for chix yadda yadda

u done enuff 4 chix

u gotta freakin henhouse ovr ther

chicks nvr appreshiate anything u do

ur complainin!

LOL

jus wait til laura sez its "her turn"

wont happen

got her sum majr bling 4 r annivrsry

she'll wear a happy face til 08

wich is y we gotta talk fast

dont want any *accidents* happenin in 08

?

58

1 word: hillary

o yeh

😲

aint no way im goin bak 2 the big wite crib

life is GOOD

& my ass is dun if u keep messin up

i told u last time wat 2 do bout harry

thats finito

didnt even need 2 off her cat like you sed

k so u got lucky

harry quit

her best legal judgment 2 date

way harsh

so how u gonna fix this nu mess

this *plamegate*

& make it quik

gotta mjr hottie waitin in my lobby

u saw wat im doin

"no comment on legl proceedins"

"now back 2 work"

"big job 2 do"

bla bla bla

that's IT?!

that's rlly ALL ur doin????

slap 4hed

u guys r so screwd

y?

scooterboy didn't do nuffin

evn the special prosecutor sed that

scoots takin the bullet 4 lyin bout it

that's it rite?

end of story

no

START of story

w Monica . . .

at least I wuz lyin bout a rlly gr8 blo job

u guys r lyin bout a rlly lame smear job

dude u shda called that plame chick
a ho flat out

rite from the start

shaken ur hed

sed "watu expct from a crazy ho like that?"

folks wdve believd it cuz shes a fox

as 4 her ol man . . .

u shda calld him a liar

BONUS POINT: he rlly wuz a liar!

& the special prosecutor

man u needed 2 take him DOWN

smear HIM real good

diss the whole vestigation

calld it a fishin expedition

sed hes sum wild dem dawg

tryin 2 bring down the presidency

in WARTIME yet

public hates that shit

they always side w the prez

but noooooo

u go & call the vestigation "serious"

u dudes cant diss worth a dam

ur DISS-abled

im gna have 2 spoonfeed u like a bunch
of babies til 08

if hills gna lose

& im 2 get any sleep.

u still ther?

😢

& in the middle of this

IN THE MIDDLE OF ALL THIS

u go piss off ur base!!!!

treatin SCOTUS like it wuz sum gold watch

2 giv 2 yr "employee of the decade"

whos givin u this advice?!

not wonderboy

can c that

u bttr stop callin those toll free lines

& pay 4 sum real help

y do u think im talking 2 u?

rite

g2g

wait

come bak

u still ther??

Auto-reply: Former president of the United States William Jefferson Clinton is not currently online. If you are interested in inviting the president to speak at an upcoming event, please go to **www.bookbill.us** for fee information and availability.

yo tony

how r u my pommy bud

hey tex

feelin a bit crook

?

u kno

sos

press takin the piss outta me

another scandal in the cabinet

1 of my best chaps goin down

how about u?

btr since thos roils left

?

ROILS

??

chuck & milly!

ah

royals

🙂

mor like roil pain in the butt

chuck askd me bout evry goddam plant in the frikkin rose gardn

tol him I dont do flowrs

jus brush

if u cant kill it or hack it up I aint intrstd

he's like "rawther describes ur iraq policy duzn't it?"

talks like sum butler

i sez dam rite

goes dwn from ther

lol

man its wrse than xmas w ur in-laws

he wont let up!

@ lunch he's like arent u wrried the planet's gettin 2 hot

im like no im wrried my burgers gettin cold

hes like the c is risin & the snows meltin!! 😲

im like por me sum mor ice t

kno wot ur sayin

he's bummy

dred him @ big functions

fllws me round like a bassett hound

"y don't we set up organic farms outside najaf?"

"y don't we rebuild baghdad like poundbury?"

"hav u considered dialog would be mor effectiv than bombs?"

like SHUT. UP.

last time we reached out to islam * hello * they bombd the tube

tru dat

67

look at r froggy bud jacques

he *reaches out*

***spirit of dialog & respect* yadda yadda**

now theyr burnin down the hood

soon itll b only muslims in paris

"muslims in paris"

sounds like a musical

wont see that 1 playin in the west end

"im singin in bahrain"

lol

wot u think of Camilla btw?

she's boo yeah

way bttr than him!!

& wat a rak!

yes wot knockrs!

no I mean RAK

as in sumthin u hang ur piece on

ur huntin piece

ive alwys thot mayb shes got a bolster in there

the way it juts strate out

yeh I wuz wrried the waiters wd mistake her 4 a servin platter

u kno jus set the drinks down on that rak

rlly

i think its more like a riting desk

we cd sign the peace accords with ireland on it

rofl

wen she stood next to my ma all i cd think of wuz 2 holsteins

wantd 2 call up my bud bono and say we'd solvd the famin in Africa

stop!! im wettin my pants

or tackl the guy with the nuke football

"stop the launch codes! the missles r pointd rite at us!!"

crikey i miss u

miss u 2 bud

we need a summit or sumpin

wuz stuk in argentina w that chavez dude

😜

u & me we're like the last tuff guys

sigh

say y dont we plan a state visit (par-tay!)

u cd com hang @ the ranch ovr xmas

or i cd chill @ checkrs

show the wrld we stik 2gether

that we're rdy 2 sav paris' ass yet agen

do the whole churchill/fdr thing

waddya say?

uh not a gd idea roit now bud

y not??

bit ruff w the party

need 2 pull bak on the *tuff guy* stuff

do sum reachin out 2 my base

man u HELP me w MY base

sry

its not the same 4 me

k

fine i ges

gna catch sum zzzs now

hang in ther bud

u2

From: President George W. Bush
Date: November 28, 2005 8:37:50 PM EST
Subject: Thanksgiving
To: Bar & Poppy

hi ma & pops

just wanted to thank you again for coming to
Crawford for thanksgiving. I know pop that you'd
wanted to spend the holiday in florida with jeb but
I appreciate you making the effort to come to us.
Also appreciated your views on how jeb would be
handling things right now vis a vis iraq although I
still think a war is a little different from a hurricane.
I'm sorry we couldn't invite your pal bill to join us
but he was busy with his family up in new york.
Besides we would've had to invite hillary and
chelsea and you know how they get along with
laura and the girls. And for sure jenna didn't need
any extra pressure on her with all of us lookin over
her boyfriend like he was some prize pig. I like
the guy—laura and i think he's settled her down a
bit—and glad you both seemed to like him too. And
ma I really wouldn't worry too much about jenna's
weight. I know you think she's touchy on the subject
but she really was embarrassed when you warned
her about seconds on the yams right in front of
her boyfriend. That's why she was so silent—she
wasn't hungover or anything. Not that she doesn't

appreciate your wisdom and advice. We all do. Barbara was just feeling sick when she got up from the table. A cold or something had been coming on all day. It had nothing to do with you telling her to giddyup on the man front or she'd be left behind jenna. Ditto for laura. No one was offended when you asked where were her jewish guests this year. She's been stressed out lately and I think she needed to lie down for the rest of the afternoon. She hardly ever eats dessert, and like you said the chef didn't make your pecan pie right. Anyway it was great to see you guys and i hope we'll all be able to do it again at xmas, if you don't decide to go to florida.

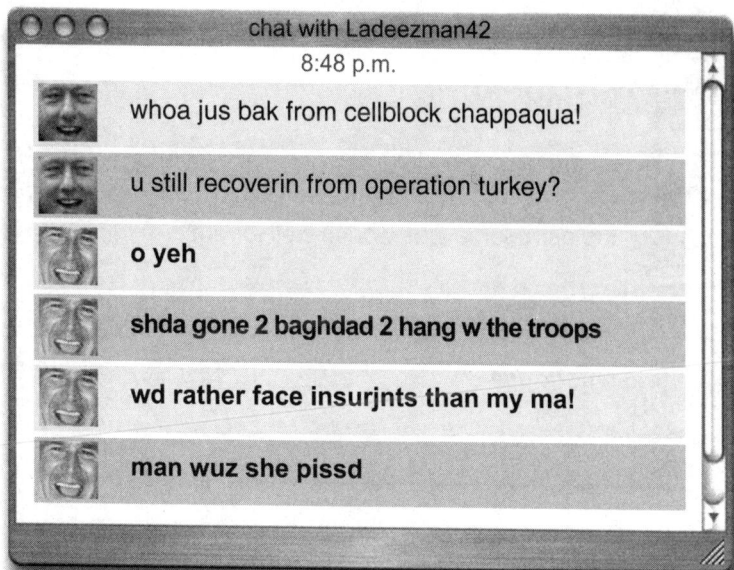

8:48 p.m.

whoa jus bak from cellblock chappaqua!

u still recoverin from operation turkey?

o yeh

shda gone 2 baghdad 2 hang w the troops

wd rather face insurjnts than my ma!

man wuz she pissd

y wuz she pissd??

she's wrryd bout evrything

sez she's seen *this* all b4

this being a bush dudes popularity tankin

rite aftr a gulf war

katrina didnt help

she took sum hits from blak folks

😂

wuz wettin my pants aftr wat she sed!

wat wuz it

"since they wuz poor anyway

the astrodome was workin well for em"

rofl

u laff dude

jus leg pullin u kid

74

ur thanxgivin cdnt hav bin worse than mine:

billy boyz in a bad way . . .

wen the only thing gettin stuffd is the turkey

i had PLANS

rlly ttlly HOT plans

sigh

?

so im like gettin off the flight from dubai rite

uh huh

my cell fone rings

its a bud from my speakr agency

theyve lined up dinner wed nite

w sum *new faces* 4 06

MODELS

☺

y wd ur agency do that?!

its ther way of sayin thanx

4 all the dough ive ben rackin up

im sposed 2 give these hot chix
career advice

like how 2 bcome interns?

lol

so im whistlin as i walk 2 my car

shakin hands w every1

fone rings agen

gess wat

wat

its hillry tellin me i gotta get my ass out 2
chappaqua *rite away*

cuz shes havin people 4 thanxgivin!!!

y didn't u jus go thurs morn

duh—thats wat i say:

chat with Ladeezman42

"so sry hon gotta meetin on wed yadda yadda"

she's like u gotta meetin wed NITE??

& i'm like no its wed AFT but its gna run l8

& I dont wanna travel wed nite

so shes like ok fine we'll meet u in town

whos "we"

XACTLY

turns out she's bin hangin w ELLEN DEGENERES

ellen degenerate?!?!

gets WRSE

theyr goin 2 a special showin of "the vagina monologs"

raisn $$$ 4 sum chix shelter or sumpin like that

did u go????

hell no

77

sed id had nuff talkin pussy

dont need no mor talkin pussy

talkin pussy jus gets me in2 trbl

u sed that?!

🫢

no

wuz leg pullin agen

i aint on no suicide mission

(wdnt mind the 72 virgins tho)

(and like y is it 72?)

(y not 37—or 105?)

dunno

theyr crzy fukrs

so wat DID u do

skedded the models in 4 lunch

then left erly 4 chappaqua

spent the nite "alone"

hil @ ell came out thurs morn

problem solvd

man thats sum thanksgiving

i jus watched dallas lose

& my ma explode

the rest wuznt so hot

playd like 100 rounds of "balderdash"
w chelsea

alwys cream her

yeh ur the balderdash mastr

im jus glad 2 be bak in dc

dont seem so bad now

compard 2 hangin w family

megadittoes

chat with Ladeezman42

btw i had anudder idea 4 u

?

did u hear that dude feingold ovr the weekend?

that cheesehed wannabe

who wants us 2 cut & run from iraq?!

bingo

lissen—act scared of the guy

get wonderboy 2 say sumpin like

"he's the 1 dude who cd beat us in 08"

giv im sum momentum

push hillary 2 the left w the crazies

& then hillary is O-U-T

got it

will think bout it

u do that

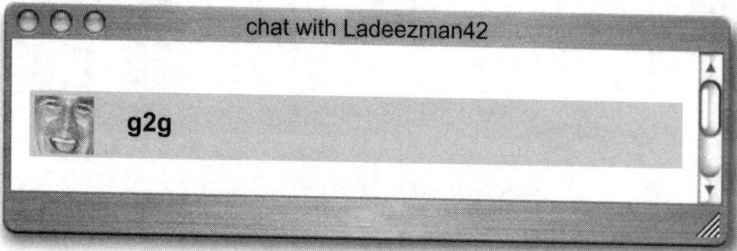

chat with Ladeezman42

g2g

Anyway it was great to see you guys and i hope we'll all be able to do it again at xmas, if you don't decide to go to florida. And hey pops, maybe Bill will be free for some of the holiday. I understand he gets kind of squirrelly up in Westchester.

W

December 6, 2006 | 9:35 a.m. (EDT)

The President Hosts a Live Discussion with Nation's Schoolchildren

For the first time in his presidency, George W. Bush will go online at 10 a.m. today to answer questions from the nation's schoolchildren. Students at selected elementary and high schools with Internet access have been chosen to participate. The discussion will be moderated by the president's counselor, Dan Bartlett.

---

chat with BigBartlett et al

9:48 a.m.

Mr. President? We'll be going on live in a few minutes. Are you ready, sir?

yep

got my odouls & sandwich

(its lunchtime 4 me!)

I will screen all the questions for you, Mr. President (i.e. there will be no surprises!) The session will last 30 minutes.

roger

chat with BigBartlett et al

We also have Karen and Condi on standby to help you as needed. You'll see I've created a chat room. If you need to IM them with a question, go ahead. No one will see the chat room. I'm doing all the official posting.

so i just im u with my answr rite?

Right, sir.

ur sure itll b private

Absolutely. You'll be able to follow the transcript of the discussion on your computer, but your answers will be posted via me. And let me say again, Mr. President, what a terrific opportunity this is to reach out to America's youth.

Get ready, sir. Here we go.

Dan Bartlett: I'd like to welcome all the students who will be participating in today's historic online discussion with the President. The President is right now sitting at his computer in the Oval Office. He is excited about answering your questions. Don't forget to let us know what grade you're in and where you're from. We'll keep your names private. So let's go.

Port Orange, Florida: Hello, Mr. President. I'm a sixth grader. My question is do you have any favorite video games? What are they?

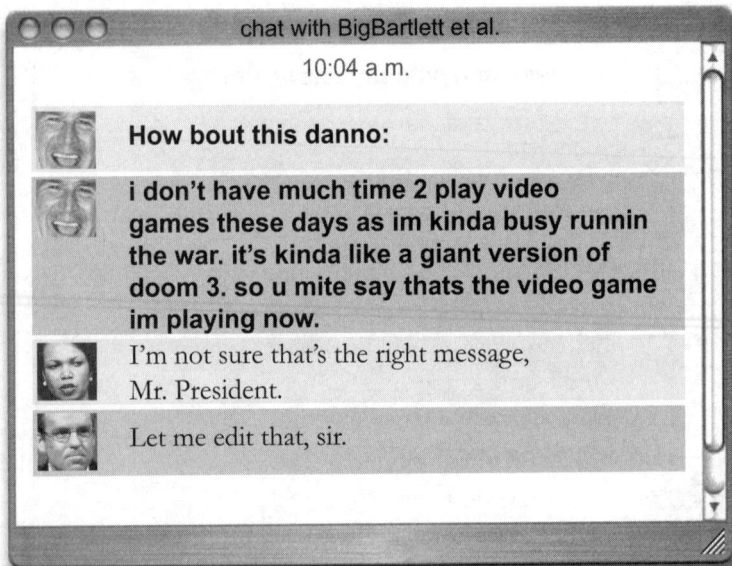

---

chat with BigBartlett et al.

10:04 a.m.

How bout this danno:

i don't have much time 2 play video games these days as im kinda busy runnin the war. it's kinda like a giant version of doom 3. so u mite say thats the video game im playing now.

I'm not sure that's the right message, Mr. President.

Let me edit that, sir.

The President: Thank you for your question. I don't have much time to play video games these days, as I'm very busy protecting our nation from terrorists and winning the war in Iraq. That's enough exciting action for anyone! But on the rare occasion when I do have time to sit down at the PlayStation with Jenna and Barbara, we like to play Madden. I just got the latest 06 version. And hey, say hello to my brother Jeb, who's working hard to improve education all across your great state.

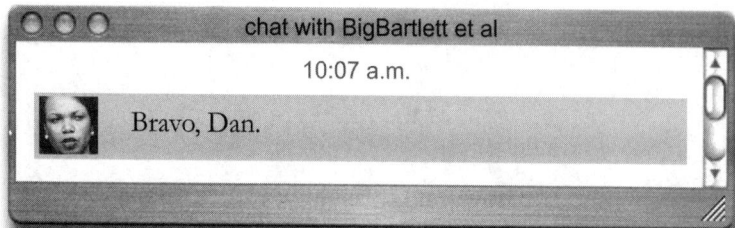

> chat with BigBartlett et al
>
> 10:07 a.m.
>
> Bravo, Dan.

Mobile, Alabama: I'm an eighth-grade African-American student and a big fan of poetry. I was pleased that you chose Maya Angelou to read a poem at the national Christmas tree lighting. What inspired you to do this?

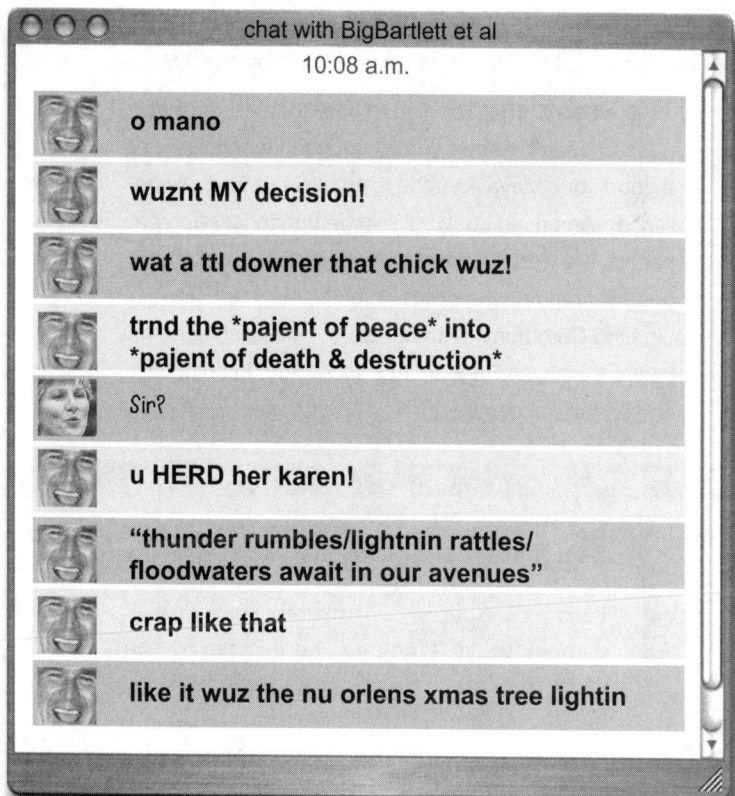

> chat with BigBartlett et al
>
> 10:08 a.m.
>
> o mano
>
> wuznt MY decision!
>
> wat a ttl downer that chick wuz!
>
> trnd the *pajent of peace* into *pajent of death & destruction*
>
> Sir?
>
> u HERD her karen!
>
> "thunder rumbles/lightnin rattles/ floodwaters await in our avenues"
>
> crap like that
>
> like it wuz the nu orlens xmas tree lightin

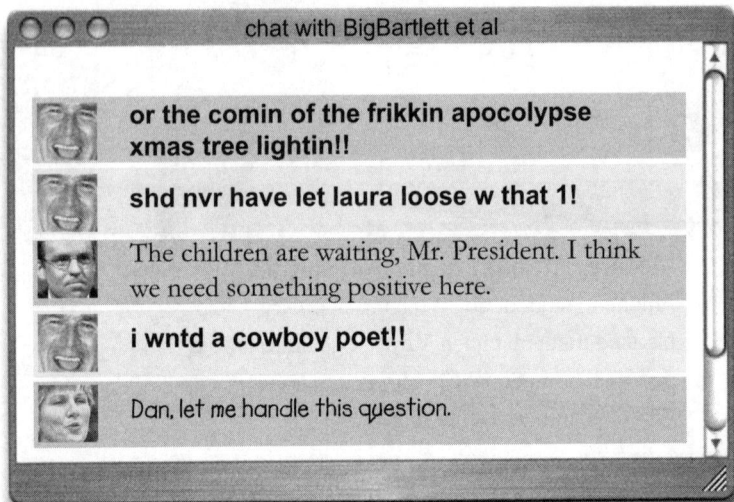

> **or the comin of the frikkin apocolypse xmas tree lightin!!**
>
> **shd nvr have let laura loose w that 1!**
>
> The children are waiting, Mr. President. I think we need something positive here.
>
> **i wntd a cowboy poet!!**
>
> Dan, let me handle this question.

The President: I'm glad to hear that you're already a fan of poetry. Shows you've got good teachers—and a good soul. Maya Angelou is not just our finest living African-American poet, but maybe our finest living poet, period. We were honored that she chose to write an original poem on the occasion of the National Tree Lighting Ceremony. With her words, she embraced this year's theme, "A Pageant of Peace." And in doing so, she embraced us all.

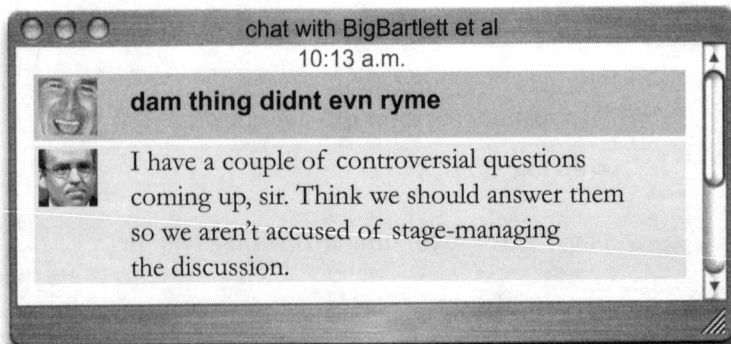

chat with BigBartlett et al

10:13 a.m.

> **dam thing didnt evn ryme**
>
> I have a couple of controversial questions coming up, sir. Think we should answer them so we aren't accused of stage-managing the discussion.

go 4 it

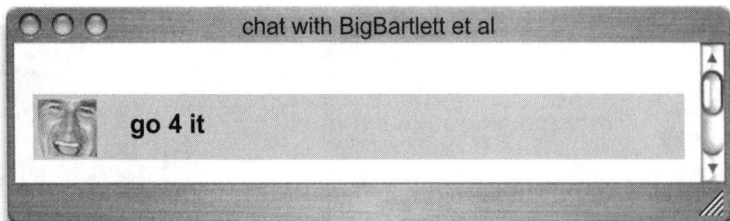

Newton, Massachussetts: I'm a middle-school student who is really upset about secret prisons and the fact that we are torturing suspects and stuff. I've been taught torture is wrong, especially when it involves my younger sister. How do you justify this?

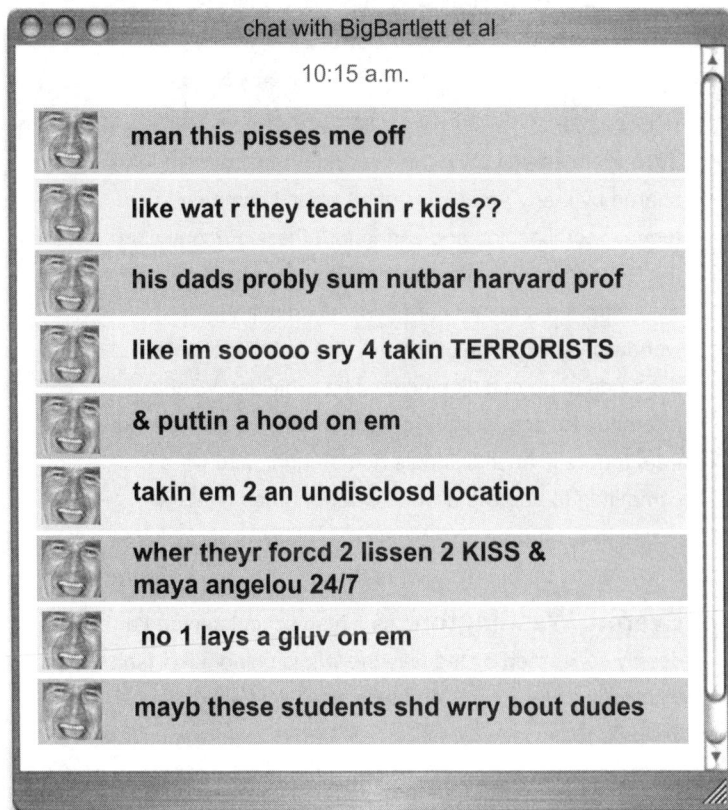

10:15 a.m.

man this pisses me off

like wat r they teachin r kids??

his dads probly sum nutbar harvard prof

like im sooooo sry 4 takin TERRORISTS

& puttin a hood on em

takin em 2 an undisclosd location

wher theyr forcd 2 lissen 2 KISS & maya angelou 24/7

no 1 lays a gluv on em

mayb these students shd wrry bout dudes

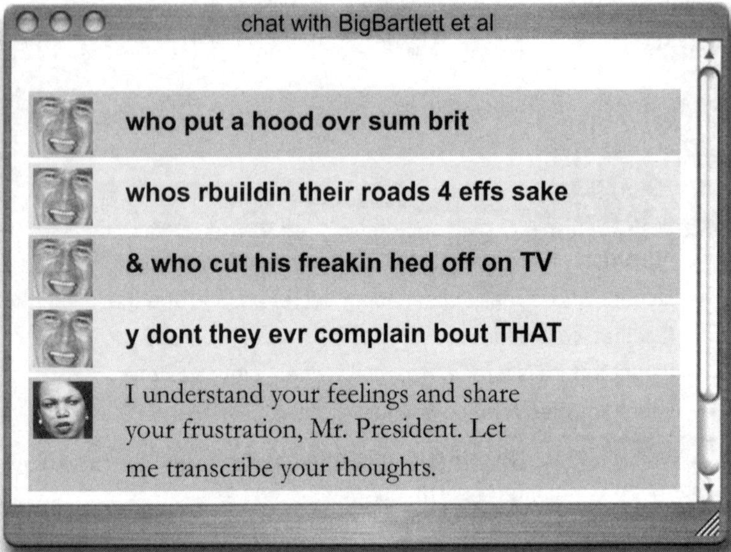
chat with BigBartlett et al
who put a hood ovr sum brit
whos rbuildin their roads 4 effs sake
& who cut his freakin hed off on TV
y dont they evr complain bout THAT
I understand your feelings and share your frustration, Mr. President. Let me transcribe your thoughts.

The President: You raise an important concern, one shared by many Americans of all ages. I commend you for your compassion and caring for others. Recently, on the United Nations International Day in Support of Victims of Torture, I reaffirmed our nation's commitment to the worldwide elimination of torture. The non-negotiable demands of human dignity must be protected without reference to race, gender, creed, or nationality. Freedom from torture is an inalienable human right, and we are committed to building a world where human rights are respected and protected by the rule of law. This includes little sisters.

Everett, Washington: As a high school senior, I am deeply concerned by the way the war is going. Like, isn't this really a war for oil? And why won't you withdraw the troops?

The President: if it wre a war 4 oil then y r gas price$ so frikkin hi?

The President: wat is it w these kids? man if ONLY it wuz a war 4 oil!

The President: then my poll #s mite b bttr!!

The President: as 4 troop withdrawl

The President: we dont lissen 2 those dem pussies

The President: who jus cut n run

The President: who don evn hav a PLAN

The President: theyr all like "we'll get 1 nxt yr"

The President: like HELLO

The President: uve had YRS 2 come up w a bttr plan

The President: but nooooo

The President: u got kerry out ther sayin r troops— R troops!—r "terrorizin" wimmin & kids

The President: he's bak in 1973 hippy attak mode

The President: like this is the best theyve got??

The President: like this wet dude nrly got electd???

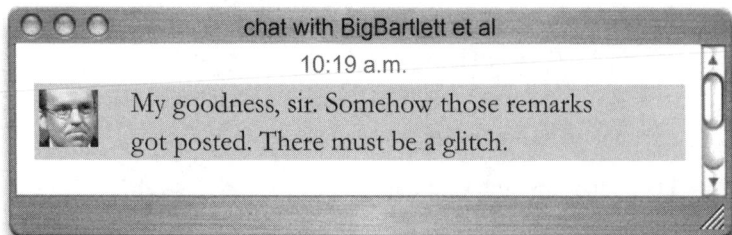

---

chat with BigBartlett et al

10:19 a.m.

My goodness, sir. Somehow those remarks got posted. There must be a glitch.

89

The President: ??

The President: 😨

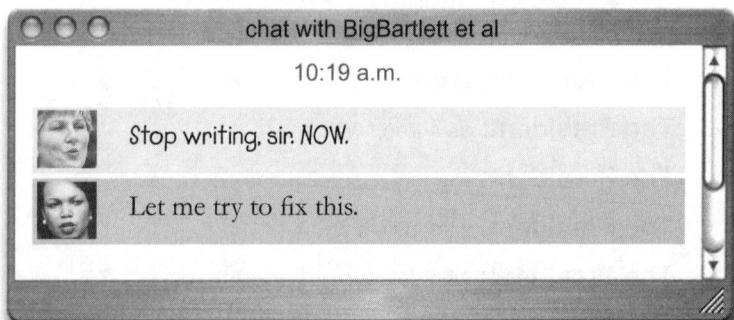

chat with BigBartlett et al

10:19 a.m.

Stop writing, sir. NOW.

Let me try to fix this.

The President: Just kidding you, Everett, Washington. Trying to show I was "hip" with the IM language. ROFL, huh? But seriously, to answer your very important question with the consideration it deserves: As we fight the enemy in Iraq, every man and woman who volunteers to defend our nation deserves an unwavering commitment to the mission—and a clear strategy for victory.

Victory in Iraq will demand the continued determination and resolve of the American people. We will not withdraw until we are persuaded we have left in place a democratic Iraq led by a federal government that is strong enough to protect minority rights.

This is not about oil. This is about freedom for Iraqis and security for all Americans.

I hope this answers your question.

Dan Bartlett: Well, it looks like we've run out of time. I'm sorry that the president will be unable to answer all of you who have sent in questions. We thank you for participating in this historic experiment. An edited transcript will be posted shortly at **www.whitehouse.gov**.

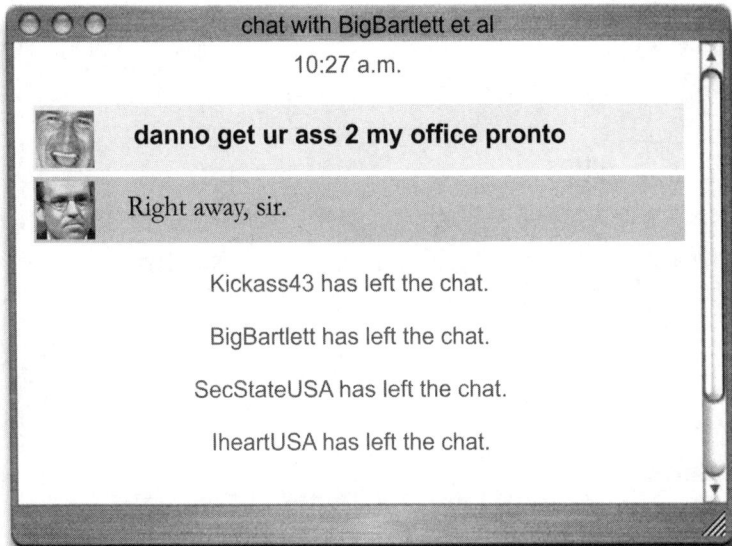

---

chat with BigBartlett et al

10:27 a.m.

danno get ur ass 2 my office pronto

Right away, sir.

Kickass43 has left the chat.

BigBartlett has left the chat.

SecStateUSA has left the chat.

IheartUSA has left the chat.

5:16 p.m.

yo

TONE

buddy boy

george II!!

merry xmas happy new year & all that bollox

dittos

ur back from the ranch already?

uh yeh

y?

rather short holiday . . . ?

often thinka u as an EU worker:

u go on strike unless you get 6 weeks off!

ha ha

mayb cuz my mom in law wuz ther

1 mor effin round of scrabble . . .

hear u

have u evr playd scrabble w schoolteachers??

im like * jo* is not a wrd

& theyr like "yes it is look it up"

im like ur bluffin

"no no look it up"

so like 10 mins l8r i find it

means "sailors girlfriend"

rlly??

no way

way

but it opens up *yo* 4 me on a triple

& theyr like "that's not a wrd"

it's "slang"

mjr eye rollin

i say look it up

wat u kno

it's ther!!

like pirates used it

theyr still eye rollin & dumpin all ovr my wrd like its not a real wrd

not like JO

twins then holler wen we wont let em use *homie*

where were UR parents?

w jeb

in an *undisclosed location*

srsly??

srsly

security?

nah

jus didnt wanna tell me

mayb dad wuz afraid I'd make im clear brush

put his back out at thanxgivin whackin a cedar

wat bout u?

took evry1 2 the red c

?

2 sharm el-sheikh

the place that got blown up??

😲

wuznt so bad

good deals roit now

all inclusive

remember—taxpayers don't pay 4 MY holiday

& no *air force 1* 4 the preem

there r 6 of us + nannies

just TRY 2 get seats 2gether @ this time of year!

95

man ur tuff

not rlly

its easier if u book ahead

cherie locked in roit after the bombings

she's canny that way

no I mean goin 2 a place like that

it wd be like me goin to new orleans 4 xmas

less local hostility in egypt i think

The user "SecretAgentMan" has sent you an Instant Message. Do you want to accept it?

Block/Accept

hold on tone

msg just poppd up from goss

Goss?!

let's form a chat room

I have SEVERAL bones 2 pick w him

chat with Sxybritguy10

won't work

his msgs 2 me r encryptd

only my computer can read em

brb

---

chat with SecretAgentMan

5:37 p.m.

=2%))000 3RT^^8` ~[LKPP^

yeh well it hasnt been so happy a nu
year 4 me eithr

%+YY2

wat secrets have ur ppl NOT told the NYT??

X*&BN]

that bttr b tru

cuz we aint gonna hav any effin allies left

if ur guys blab we hav secret camps
in poland

lefty wingnuts actin like weve rebilt treblinka

euroweenies dissin the poles like sum mean girl posse

NICE JOB

im sure this is how r buds expectd 2 b thankd 4 their contributions 2 the war

/4LSI*(]]2HY%^ *HK—~CC

B./S ?\ { FFTY6^

🙁

we'll c

then thers all this wiretappin crap

ur leakin like the frikkin titanic

thanx 2 u we've managd 2 combine vietnam & watergate in a single newz cycle!

agen:

NICE JOB

@O{ KL"(U%GJI>>L FGH%^NB JSKLP= MSKP~JSP[08

dude it aint gettin bttr

xplain this 2 me:

scootys indictd 4 "outing" a retired CIA soccer mom

he gets wrse press than the freakin rosenbergs

but leakin the locations of secret prison facilities

& revealin 2 al qaeda how we're listenin 2 em

is like OK??

|0*YH #F?LKJJ !~K(BN^

man i didn't xpect u 2 xplain it

i xpect u 2 FIX it

u got ur own insurgency goin on ovr in langley

i cant deal w any mor of em

ur on ur own

clean out ur nest of enemy spies

SN279[&^PLK){ } + BHL"_)*HG

if u cant lick a buncha deskhumpin speeddiallin squealin soccer moms

we sure aint lickin the terrorists

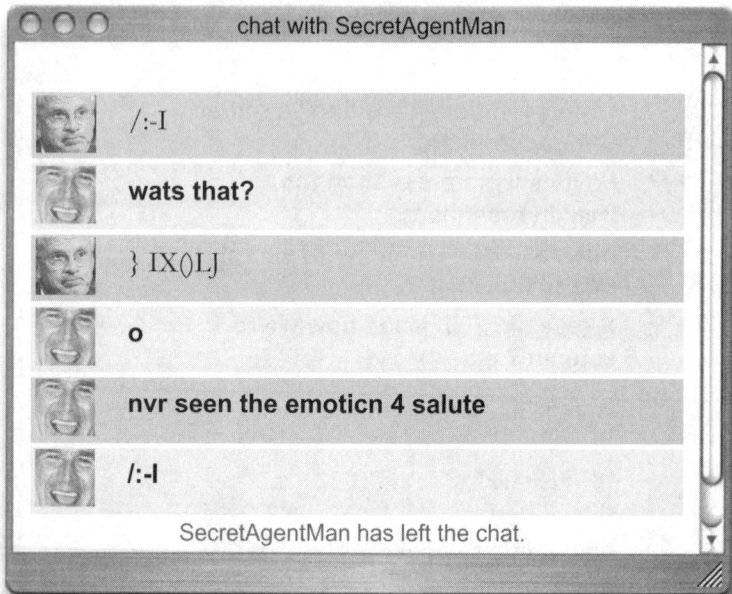

chat with SecretAgentMan

/:-I

wats that?

} IX()LJ

o

nvr seen the emoticn 4 salute

/:-I

SecretAgentMan has left the chat.

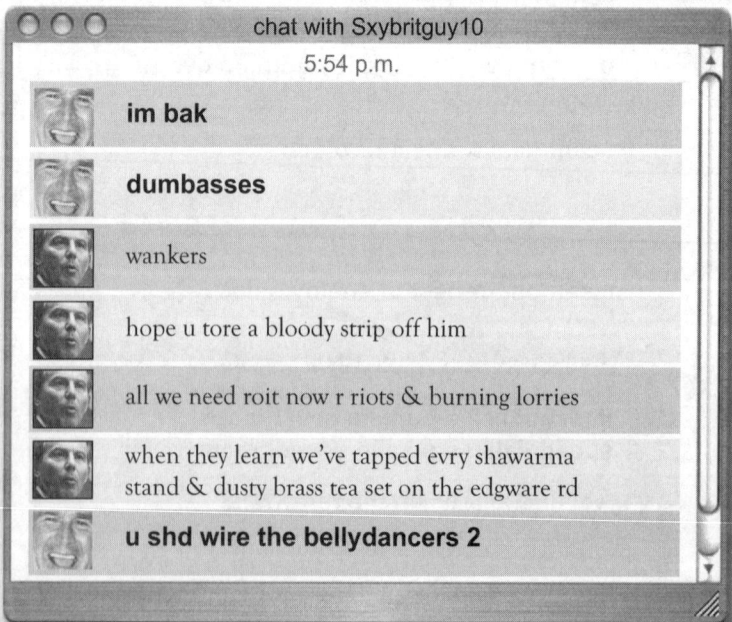

chat with Sxybritguy10

5:54 p.m.

im bak

dumbasses

wankers

hope u tore a bloody strip off him

all we need roit now r riots & burning lorries

when they learn we've tapped evry shawarma stand & dusty brass tea set on the edgware rd

u shd wire the bellydancers 2

tried it—poor reception

& it keeps falling out of their navels

lol

so wats ur resolution 4 this yr?

just 2 get thru it frankly

me 2

sumtimes wen im wrestlin cedar i think of wat its gonna be like when this is all ovr

didnt like 2 think of it b4

now i cant wait 4 08

wot u gna do?

gna kick bak @ the ranch

aint gonna b no world travelin xprez

tryin 2 drum up sum peace prize

reagan got it rite

coz he retired 2 CA?

nope

cuz he f4got evrything

sounds good 2 me

happy nu year bud

u2

chat with Kickass43 et al

7:02 a.m.

Mr. President?

Everyone you asked for is assembled in the chat room.

We're ready to go over the final draft of SOTU.

Are you there, sir?

yep

I suspect you're much happier with this version.

wdve liked mor jokes

ppl like jokes

1st 10 mins is all "thank u"s

like thank u senatr this

thank u senatr that

thank u so&so 4 showin up

COURS they showd up

hottest tickt in the capital

after coldplay

Yes, sir.

so we need sum 1 liners rite off the top

get folks warmd up

Well—you know what Karl says about humor

"The president should be funny but not too funny."

It's not late-night TV.

is 4 me!

starts @ 9!

whers wonderboy anyway?

hes not listd in the chat room

He'll be joining us for the practice session later, Mr. President.

☹

You'll see we were able to make all the changes you asked for, sir.

xept cda

Canada is there, sir. Page 8.

Para beginning: All over the world, new democracies are emerging. I am proud to stand here and announce tonight that after twelve years of one-party rule, democracy has finally blossomed in our neighbor to the north. [pause for applause]

snot wat i wantd danno

if u recall i wantd sumpin strongr

not jus the democracy crap

sumpin that gives us mor credit 4 gettin ridda ther corrupt regime

unlike frikkin palestine

wher we givem the frikkin vote

& they elect a gang of frikkin terrorists

man they wernt usin no purpl ink ovr ther

they were stickin ther fingers in blood

If I may weigh in here, Mr. President.

I was the one who toned down the Canada stuff.

Even though Mr. Harper won the election, his conservatives are still a minority

that sooo burns

Yes. Thus Mr. Harper will have to govern cautiously, working with the other parties. It's almost like the coalition situation we have in Iraq.

yeh xept theyr not workin w shiites & sunnis

I see you haven't had many dealings with the Quebecois.

chretien wuz bad enuff!

he cdnt talk english OR french

& man thos cdn frenchies!

evr eaten quebec grub steve?

Haven't had that honor yet, sir.

they srvd it 2 me in ottawa

😄

im like "excusez-moi but cd I hav my steer w/out cheez curdz merci bocoo?"

theyr like "porkwa?"

In any case, sir, we now have the opportunity to reopen dialogue with a new Canadian leader . . .

on all kinds of issues . . .

not least the oil sands they've discovered
in northern Alberta . . .

that contain potentially as much oil as
in Saudi Arabia.

?

!

In short, Mr. President, it wouldn't be prudent
to take too much credit for the Harper
government's success at this time.

Indeed, I thought you might want to make
some mention of your desire to come to
some agreement over softwood lumber.

Not a commitment, of course—just a
suggestion that you're open for business.

dialogue.

whoa steve

still reelin here

as much oil as in Saudi Arabia

☺

wahoo!

107

so like—screw ANWAR?!?!

Something like that, sir. If they can extract the oil from the sand, which is not an easy process.

wait

r ther like any cute baby animals who live near the oil sands?

big eyed baby seals?

fluffy wite polar bers??

noble elk ???

Not so far as I know, sir. Just mosquitoes.

I should say BIG mosquitoes.

In some countries mosquitoes of that size would count as wildlife.

But not even Canadians feel protective of their bugs, sir.

sweet

So we're agreed we'll keep the language on Canada as is, Mr. President?

k fine

rite in wat steve sez on lumbr

next

Condi here, sir.

hi 5 GF!!

u ROCKD the mideast!

rlly kickd ass

LUVd ur tuff talk bout hamas

btw

1st lady & I miss YA!

Thank you, Mr. President.

I just have one quick point.

I think we need to insert something more into the speech about the Palestinian elections.

I'm glad we noted the historical importance of these elections.

But I think we have to be careful about saying what we will do or won't do in the future.

We should even sound hopeful about the democratic process.

o rite

wat bout: "long alienatd from the democratic process, suicide bombrs will finally b representd in an electd parliament"

or: "insted of traditional firewrks joyous votrs torchd govt bldgs & led pogroms in jeroosalem . . ."

I know you're surprised and even angry about this, sir.

We all are.

Who knew?

But for better or worse we are going to have to engage with the newly elected Hamas government—

?!

c-grl u jus kickd hamas ass

& now u want ME 2 *engage* w em?

I don't mean engage right now. I mean lay the groundwork for future engagement, which I'm afraid is going to be inevitable. Nothing too strong.

o no GF

ur goin native on me

i knew it!!!

I beg your pardon, Mr. President?

i wondrd how long it wuz gna take b4 colin got 2 u

I honestly don't know what you're implying, sir.

& that dude chirac: he jus oozes greasy charm dont he

o yes the euros jus LUV condi in her sxy suits & her stormtroopr boots

SecStateUSA has left the chat.

Mr. President, I believe we should address the Secretary of State's very valuable point.

fine!

nada $$$ 4 r terrorist amigos

dont care if they win the effin caucuses in iowa

they aint gettin no moola from us

aint talkin 2 em neither

till they renouns violens

Mr. President, if I may just weigh in here for a moment.

go ahed karen

As your undersecretary of state to the Islamic world . . .

you know how many inroads I have made personally . . .

into the hearts and minds of Islamic women and children . . .

I was swarmed wherever I traveled . . .

by darling little girls in hair ribbons . . .

their mothers in hijab . . .

determined to tell me that their mullahs who spewed such hatred toward us . . .

did not speak for them.

Indeed, they wanted me to understand that they don't hate us . . .

to truly, really, honestly understand that . . .

and also to give them Bic pens.

wats ur point??

I agree with Condi that we can't simply slam the door on the Palestinian people just because they elected a gang of murderous thugs.

I think the wording as we have it now will do, Mr. President. We'll just repeat your language about not sponsoring or engaging with any state that supports terrorism and leave it to Condi to figure out how we're going to get around it.

not

now wat bout SCOTUS?

i askd 4 an alito victry lap

rally the base

now that *hurricane harry* has blown ovr

we're battin 2 fer 2!

Funny you should mention it, sir.

I DID insert a section about our success with the Supreme Court nominations . . .

and yet when copies of the speech were made, those parts were mysteriously excised.

I just noticed that it's missing from this draft too.

HMiers has left the chat.

I'll make sure that gets put back in. I'll make the copies myself.

jus 1 mor thing danno

durin rehersal cd u talk 2 the veep?

tell im he needs 2 wrk on his *listenin face*

he jus sits ther kinda slumpd bhind me

like hes had anudder heart attak

mouth open

eyes rolld up

recks the mood

giv im a spicy burrito or sumpin jus b4 the speech

Yes, Mr. President.

chat with Ladeezman42

10:07 p.m.

yo

u ther dude?

yeh

so wat?

u talkin 2 me?

y dya care?

thot U wernt talkin 2 ME

man im ALWYS talkin 2 u

ur still the main man

& i prechiated yr wrds

in last wks SOTU

wen u sed "my ol mans 2 favrite ppl—me & Bill Clinton"

man that took guts

bet ur bro jeb wuz surprizd

dude thats y i sed it

u & my ol man r like BFFs

all my freakin life im like:

wat do i gotta do 4 my ol man 2 like me bttr than jeb??

he sez: stop bein a badass

so i stop bein a badass

go on 2 bcome 2-term prez

kick saddams ass

all the time drink nuffin strongr than a freakin buckler

evn on 9/11

& whose his biggst BFF now . . . ?

U!!

biggst badass EVR

sux

so y u tell the world

if it sux so much?

cuz it pisses off jeb

bsides the ol man told me 2 thank u

4 all the katrina stuff

bla bla bla

sry dude

but we're still buds rite?

🙂

i need u man!!

thot u didnt

now that hllry's soooo bhind in the race 4 08

ur badass is safe

no need 2 make me look gd no mor

u gotta go help ur ol bud gore

he's the moveon.org king now

wat a joke

the only reason that dude's still walkin

is cuz hes solar-powerd by that bald spot on his hed

at nite they gotta tuck his robotic ass away

save on batteries

lol

glad i can still make u laff bud

cuz i gotta big problem

mayb u can help

ur ol man cdnt

kno ur busy

w mideast blowin up etc.

uh yeh

kinda

i RLLY need ur help w sumpin

?

k so its v-day nxt wk rite?

uh oh

4got!

😮

ur a happly married man

til nxt wk

rite

so I had PLANS

suite @ 4 seasons

champagne/ flowers/ chocolates

rez @ smokin hot restaurant

wow!

all this 4 hill?

not HLLRY!

😦

119

chat with Ladeezman42

man this wuz 4 my GF

or shd i say my GF 2 b

o

;)

so heres my PROBLEM

hill calls

she's all *kissy kissy*

"so wat r we doin 4 v-day hon?"

xoxoxoxo

i'm like scratchin my hed

i cant REMEMBR spendin v-day w her

like not 4 a decade

(xept post-monica

had 2 buy her a negligee)

yeh yeh

then the litebulb goes on

man shes in troubl

T-R-O-U-B-L

shes cozyin up 2 me 2 pleez the base!

she wants that lovey dovey foto op w dear ol bill

hek she NEEDS u man

i did NOT book a table @ nyc's hottest 2 share w hllry!

wat am I gna do??

ur a married man!

tell me!

SOS!

dunno

bin a LONG time since i spent v-day w a GF

& u kno laura:

shes happy w takeout & an ol john wayne movie

uh rite

wantd 2 ask ur ol man wat 2 do

but hes not cool w the GF stuff

he'd tell me 2 spend it w hllry

dya kno wat hllry wants 2 do?

dude I don't lissen in on EVRYBODY

get this:

she's snaggd sum donors plane

wants 2 wing down 2 littl rok

"jus the 2 of us"

hav sum bbq at r ol roadside joint

c the "ol haunts"

"reignite the magic"

ew

xactly

meanwile I cd b w a supermodel

sloshin bak krug

in my sweet suite

man!

do I LOOK like I still eat BBQ?

thats tuff

but cant help u

havent bin ther

but *feel ur pain*

how??

u jus sed u nvr bin ther

yeh but chicks r always stoppin me from wat i want 2 do

theyr alwys reckin my plans

U??!

gimme jus 1 e.g. church boy

k

so these islamo nutbars r flippin out rite?

cuz of like a CARTOON

uh huh

the riots hav SYRIA all ovr em

theyr burnin the frog flag in damascus

not jus the danes flag

wats that bout rite?

ur point . . . ?

its all bout syria!

theyr @ it agen!!

so I sez 2 condi:

lets jus take these dudes out once & 4 all

man theyr so TINY

not like iran rite?

lets jus take em out

BAM!

u mean take out SYRIA?

yeh

y not?

uh becuz its like a WHOLE country??

u mean a shit hole country

anyhoo condi's like: that's not a gd idea rite now sir

im like: so wen?

& condis like: not now

& im like PLS

& shes like: im not ready 2 go that far yet

& im like: so wen will u b?

& shes like: i dunno

its sooooo frustratin!!!

feel UR pain bud

tho i nvr wantd 2 take out a country

jus a hot babe

o thats rite

4got u r *aspirin factry man*

boo hoo!

i mite hit sum1!!

hey dont knok it

lets c u b mr. popular wen u leave office

tooshay

so wat u gna do re hllry?

sigh

dunno

mayb u can get me a rez @ the hottest restaurant in copenhagen?

send me ovr as a *special envoy*

heal the wounds?

sry

ur 2 late

where dya think my ol man wants 2 take my ma?

😠

hey heres a plan

helps me 2

dems bin pushin 4 a WH briefin on this NSA crap

y dont i invite sum top senators 2 a *supersecret* briefin at the WH

on Feb 14?

🙂

bout 7 pm?

done

wat bout laura?

it IS v-day

how u gna hav a romantic dinner w senators hangin in ur crib?

no problemo

harry can do the briefin

miers?

she'd luv it

bsides she'd jus b hangin round laura & me on v-day

complainin souter hasnt calld

lemme tell u sumpin bout chix

they CARE bout v-day

nah

not laura

shes cool

she dont xpect no candles & luv u 4ever crap

ur so rong

they ALL do

128

no matter wat they say

they want the teddy bear floral arrangemnts

& sumpin that sparkles

rlly??

rlly

sumpin thatll blind her in the sun

hmm

well I WUZ gna get her that 4 her birthday

but mayb ur rite

cd do it 4 v-day

is it rlly rlly big?

its HUGE man

its a nu brush saw!

uh

wuz thinkin sumpin mor in the bling dept

nah

I KNO she'll prefer the brush saw

ok

ur the boss

I'll b toastin u w bubbly from gothem

u btter b bud

u owe me big time now

☺

8:07 p.m.

giorgio!

"yo"

"dood"

hey sylvio!

its like 2 am ur time

wuz gna call u 2mrrow

say grazie 4 all ur hospitality 2 mrs. b @ the olympix

iz not 2 late 4 me amico

the partys still goin

4give me if I boast but . . .

ur missus had fabulous time

she wazza de toast of turino

& mite I add

she has a lvly figure

well like I sed:

grazie 4 all that

we'll catch up soon

I think ur lady enjoyed very much de snowboarding

uh huh

& also de luge

gr8

her visit 2 de local hospital . . .

wazza vry well receivd

k

no offens bud

but its kinda crzy here rite now

mayb we cd chat sum othr time . . . ?

ah!

4giv me

you are leadr of wrld superpowr!

no time 2 "chill" wid ur lttl NATO buds

its not like that

rlly

APPRESHIATE ur friendship & support

& r troops in iraq

yes!

I donta like 2 complain

but my ppl donta like it

(diz iraq bizness)

of course dey donta understand de
affairs offa de wrld

i kno it

& APPRESHIATE it

jus sayin ive got sum problems @ the mo

problemos

VENTE problemos

gotta deal w em

c c

I understand

although mine r not big . . .

I hav summa my own problemos here atta home

bhind in polls

& 3 ladies 2 satisfy on st. valentine's day

after swearin offa sex till da election

april 9!

datsa 7.5 mor weeks

54 days

. . .

1296 hours

uomo!

I wish my problems wuz jus polls

man IF ONLY it wuz polls

I MISS wen it wuz jus polls

yes I red ur unfortunate news

dat shooting bizness wid signor cheney

actually dat iz y I'm "IM-ing"

itta waz de talk of de party

watta dis dood whittington kno?

whittington?

kno?

c

surely summathing vry important

4 ur vice president 2 pop him

dude!

dick didn't POP him

it wuz an ACCIDENT

jus a lttl casual accident tween buds!!

iva misunderstood

i thotta he sprayd summa ol man w/bullets

& tried 2 cvr it up

thats wat the MEDIA is sayin

im so sry 2 hear it

inna my country

esp sicilia

we kno how 2 do a hit

widout da press knowin

& r polizia:

😳

not like that!

wuz no problem w the "polizia"

happnd in tx

they were huntin

jus HUNTIN

& like the ranch owner

an ol family bud

w ol family $$

goes & squeals!

issa vry bad news

& now u musta take dissa *bud* out also?

repeat: not like that

evry1s makin such a dam fuss

wuz jus birdshot!

but nooooo

ther I am

sunday aft

chillin w barney in the big wite crib

watchin USA kick ass @ turin

& wunderin how 2 wrap the brush
saw i got 4 laura 4 v-day

all offa suddn

fones jumpin

"we've gotta problem mr. president"

like its apollo 13

I did not see dat film

nvr mind

its BAD

& like lauras ovr ther

lunchin w the pope!!

so much 4 his prayrs

benny issa no JP2

veeps callin evry 2 secs

actin like he's gonna hav anudder hrt attak

hm

y "hm"?

I thinka I c da problem:

ur man cheney issa man of honor correct?

DUH

u kno that

c c

so mayb dis whittington dood insulted him

or prhaps hissa wife??

lissen up silvio

dick didn't do this on purpose

whittingtons like a MJR fundraisr

mucho $$$

AND hes a tuff ass

HES not talkin 2 the press

xcept 2 say from the hospital

that it wuz an honor & privilej 2 be shot by the veep

v impressive

still . . .

makes no sense

let me try 2 follow:

dick pops summa guy

PLS

NOT pops

ok

so his hit goes wrong

NOT hit

huntin accident

ok

dis "huntin accident"

c

widda mjr fundraisr

c

who knowsa nothing

C

is leakd 2 da press by a rich lady

who goes a waya bak wid de family

u got it

she's "hot" dissa lady?

shes ok

blond chick

ha!

den dere issa only 1 conclusion my amico

?

dis wuzza crime of passion!

?!

watta other motive cd dis chick have 2 betray ur man dick?

y did dick hav 2 shoot da dude whittington?

becuzza: dey were in luv wid da same woman!

BUT

dissa woman did not luv dick

SO

wen he shot her tru luv whittington

she wuzza upset

THUS

she squealed

as u say inna english:

"de fat lady hassa begun her cantata"

Dick. Cheney.

crime of passion

hahahahahahahahahahaha

y u laff?

ur jokin rite

I don't c "joke"

dude he's like 65

im 69!!

& he's gotta mjr hrt condition

inna luv we all suffr mjr conditions of da heart

& the dude he blows is like 78

perfecto!

bottom line: he's DICK CHENEY

trust me

dis reeks offa passion

ulla c

uh ok

i'll take ur wrd bud

now I got me a brush saw 2 wrap

merciful madre of God

a brush saw!

wat u get urra mistress?

a duck blind?!

ha ha ha

NOT funny dude

thats wat dick got lynne

chat with Party_gurl

12:03 p.m.

daddy!

hey jen

wazzup punkin

im liek soooo pissd

im liek rlly pissd

?

u wdnt believe it

wat

its so OUTRAJUS

sweetiepie

ur dads kinda busy

pls get 2 the pt

well liek SORRY

but summa us hav problems 2 K?

liek im ur baby gurl

& this is ttlly majr

sry 2 b impashunt

but ive got the sheik of dubai IMing me

hes super p.o.'d

not as pissd as me!!!!!!!!!!!

look @ this!! http://www.misseducation.com/

12:08 p.m.

are you still there, your Excellency?

sry ur hiness

sumthin droppd on my desk

im here

a thousand pardons, mr. president!

Everyone in the world wants your ear

and yet you have only two.

146

i was only just saying

that his Excellency your esteemed father

was a true friend

im ur bud 2 ur hiness

kuwait was magnificent

I jus need sum time

it was our pleasure to donate $1 million

to the erection of his library

and yet so inadequate a gesture

given what he did for our people

but we do what we can for our friends.

the family rlly appreshiatd it

and his Excellency the esteemed
President Clinton

such a true friend also!

to miss an opportunity to blow up
that miserable dog bin laden

so as not to risk killing any members of our royal families

with whom he may have been falconing at the time.

a true, true friend.

and "entre nous"

how nobly he endures

that burden god inflicted upon him as a wife!

i have told him numerous times that should he choose to retire

at one of our many five-star world-class luxury resorts

"The best golf on the gulf"

and undergo a small conversion

he could have as many beautiful wives as he chooses!

of course you are a great friend of ours as well—

which makes this nasty and unfortunate business over the dubai ports

that much more painful.

12:21 p.m.

DADDY

Hel-LO

liek r u evn lissenin 2 me??????

hon i don't have time 2 chk that link

wat duz it say?

its a PLAY

bout ME

"The Miss Education of Jenna Bush"

In the comedy, the president's notoriously rebellious daughter—having just awoken from a blowout kegger—prepares for her new job teaching fourth graders on the eve of her first day at school. From underage drinking citations and (alleged) pot smoking to America's public school system, "Miss Jenna" rewrites history with a lesson plan you'll never forget.

gr8 hon!

im so proud

u shd b proud 2

149

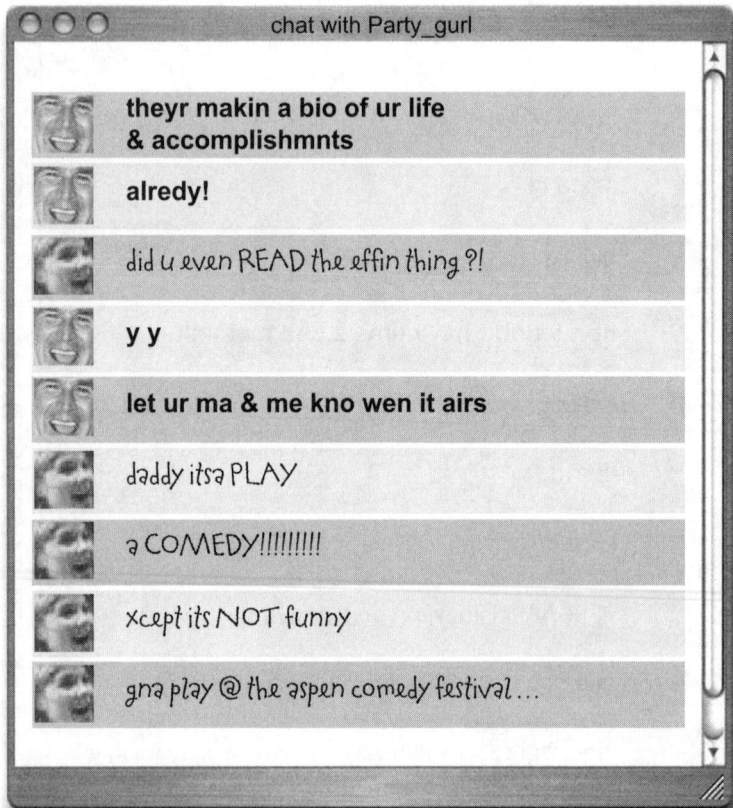

chat with Party_gurl

theyr makin a bio of ur life & accomplishmnts

alredy!

did u even READ the effin thing ?!

y y

let ur ma & me kno wen it airs

daddy itsa PLAY

a COMEDY!!!!!!!!!

xcept its NOT funny

gna play @ the aspen comedy festival ...

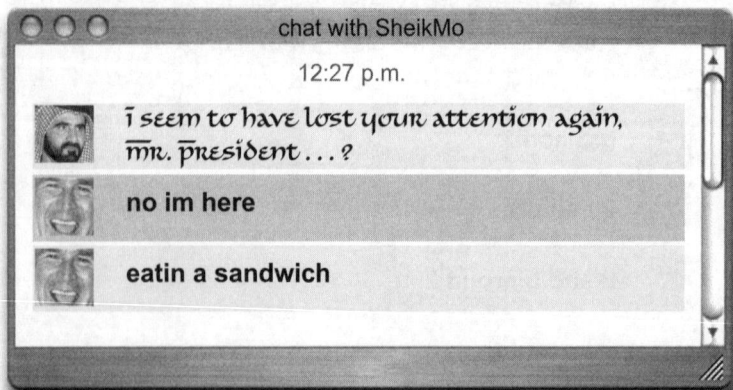

chat with SheikMo

12:27 p.m.

i seem to have lost your attention again, mr. president ... ?

no im here

eatin a sandwich

a BIG sandwich

sumtimes gets in the way of the screen

forgive me if i say that you americans

do not know how to enjoy the pleasantness

of a leisurely lunch.

imagine the leader of the greatest world power history has ever known

eating at his desk!

may i also say that it is bad for the digestion

to eat in this rushed fashion.

in any case, mr. president

i was only remarking that

his Excellency the esteemed president Clinton

was just in Qatar again.

he is such a favorite of the royal family

a hero

it is generous of you to describe him as such.

we of course view him the same way.

no

im EATIN a hero

thats wat we call big sandwiches

how amusing of americans to use the same word for a sandwich

that they also use to describe the courageous troops

who have so selflessly shed blood and given their lives

for those few arab friends and allies

who believe in the great western causes of freedom

and democracy

and free trade.

let us not forget also how many uae heroes

have shed blood and given their lives in this cause.

i shur don't 4get it sheik

& the merikan ppl dont 4get it

you know the hearts and minds of your people so well.

that is why, if i may say, all this unpleasantness over the ports

is so surprising.

such generous people!

such big people!

such "heroes"!

and yet that unfortunate strain of bigotry

that runs through your society

just below the surface

like a vein of oil beneath the sands

occasionally exploding with tragic consequences

i worry greatly, your Excellency, is at work here

undermining our port deal.

i can ashur u ur hiness

its not "bigotry"

(tho sumtimes useful 2 call it that)

its FEAR

the dems hav scared the shit outta ppl

youd think al qaeda wuz gna b inspectin the containers!

i was unaware this doctor frist was a "dem" as you put it?

And are not other Republicans joining in the general enragement?

uh yeh

summa them dont like it

democracy is a great gift to humanity.

Truly, Your Excellency, i believe that.

but in times of national crisis

it is helpful for the leaders of a society

to present a unified front to the people.

Certainly no one in our world

154

chat with SheikMo

would dare to question the decisions of the rulers

especially as they know we make all our decisions

based on the example of the prophet himself

who always did what was good and merciful for his people.

Can you not silence these outspoken party members?

chat with Party_gurl

12:43 p.m.

DADDY U HAFTA STOP THIS!!

im DYIN

dya hav any idea how BAD THIS IS?

SOS!!!

pls can we talk l8r??

WEN

2nite?

come 4 dinnr

cant

hav plans

meetin my posse after wrk

so come aftr

cant

we're all goin 2 Play

if its *soooo* srious

cant u play anudder time??

ur so outta it

"Play" is a CLUB

ull be asleep

i need u 2 fix this NOW

jen I don't hav time 2 talk bout this!!

u can stop it!

HOW

ur liek the PRESIDENT

itsa stupid low life comdy fest

pull ther grant!

nuke em!!

I DON'T CARE

pls IM ur ma

i did alrdy

she can't help

she only duz book fests

sed 2 ask u

giv me sum time

how much?!

l8r

but i have been going on at great length.

i fear by your silence that i may have caused offense.

i know there can be no truer friend to us than your excellency

the president of the mighty united states.

i think of america's mightiness every time

i have the occasion to ride upon

one of our national airline's american-made boeings

as opposed to the airbuses made by france.

yes, we could have saved millions by purchasing them instead.

and the airbus is not an inferior aircraft, as you know.

although i hasten to add it is not a boeing.

but the french are such unreliable friends!

and naturally we must preserve our greatest hospitality

and patronage

for our truest friends.

no offens takn ur hiness

& I appreshiate ur patience

& patronaj

jus need mor time

a lttl more time

2 solv this "storm ina port"

heh heh

u can rly on me

im the PRESIDENT 4 effs sake

We don't forget that, Your Excellency.

And we won't forget it, Your Excellency.

SheikMo has left this chat.

chat with Wonderboy et al

4:19 p.m.

The chat room is ready for you, Mr. President.

u got rove?

I'm here.

Let me begin by congratulating you, sir, for standing up against bigotry . . .

in our party, our opposition, and indeed our nation . . .

over the Dubai port deal.

It sent an important message to our Arab allies:

"We care about your contribution to the War on Terror."

"We stand by you."

Even if Congress wouldn't stand by us.

yeh well rite now r msg sux

karl ur the rockt scientist

how dya xplain it???

Explain what specifically, sir?

the big stax of mumbo jumbo

u dumpd on my desk

pi chartz/bar grafs/stats

man it looks like greenspans new bio

That would be the new Consumer Confidence Index.

i KNO

it sez that on pg 1!

Why don't I just walk over to your office & go thru it with you, sir.

I've included some of our new internal polling data as well.

thats NOT the part i need xplaind

Which aspect of the data is unclear?

NUN of its *unclear*

its all 2 clear!

job growth: UP

wages: UP

economy: UP

"strongest in more than two years"

home heatin costs: DOWN

In summary: The University of Michigan's current conditions index, which reflects Americans' perceptions of their financial situation and whether it's a good time to buy big-ticket items like cars, rose to 106.2 from 105.6 last month. Job growth and rising wages are helping to fuel the consumer spending that's powering a rebound in growth this quarter.

do i need 2 go on??

Karl and I are aware of the figures, Mr. President.

We are thrilled for you.

Your agenda to grow a vibrant economy...

while protecting American workers and families...

and securing the future for our nation's children and seniors...

has proven a success by every standard.

Ditto, sir.

Message: The economy is strong and continues to grow.

Was that all?

NO

heres the part i dont get:

approvl ratins: DOWN

supprt 4 irak: DOWN

congressional approvl: DOWN

"direction of country": DOWN

direction of effin UNIVERS: DOWN!!

merikans r drivin/eating/shoppin/drinkin

pimpin ther rides

trickin out ther cribs

takin ther frikkin mistresses 2 vegas

& i get NOOOOO credit!!

aint fair!!

clinton cld turn the oval office in2
a bordello

pvt humidor

get IMPEACHD

but so long as the gd times rolld

his peeps LUVD him!

xplain THAT!

I agree it's confusing, sir.

I've been running the numbers on this

4get the nos!

we need a NU msg

+++ msg

get attention on the economy

& away from irak

I couldn't agree more, sir.

Something like "Hope Thrives in Our Economy."

We could arrange for some op-eds:

164

"Women, Children, Muslims benefit from improved economic outlook."

"Muslims," Karen?

Please explain.

I'm just thinking out loud here, but yes, Muslims.

Housing starts are at a record high, isn't that right, Karl?

Yes.

So why don't we find some Muslim families who are building new homes . . .

in irak?!

No, sir. Here. In Virginia.

Or even better: in New Orleans.

"A Muslim family rebuilds the American dream after Katrina."

We could make it a photo-op!

Send you down there, sir.

Shirtsleeves. Ball cap.

There ARE a lot of new housing starts in New Orleans.

"The Salim family thanks President Bush for the economy that has made building their dream home—and finding Mr. Salim a new job—possible."

Message: Despite death and destruction elsewhere, Islam flourishes here at home.

You might want to modify that message slightly, Karen.

like its not flurishin @ r ports

Or our borders.

or r air termnls

Or basically at any neighborhood near you.

How about "safely flourishing"?

uh uh

wont play

With all due respect, Karen, I don't think this is the "big" message

the administration is currently seeking.

"Muslims prospering from Bush policies" is not a message that will please our base.

And we NEED to please our base.

Now.

Right away.

Exactamundo.

Let me run this idea by you, sir.

Our focus group research shows that while your policies remain popular

they become unpopular when associated with certain members of your administration.

So just to be hypothetical here, the public might support a "general plan to grow apples" but will oppose a "Cheney or Rumsfeld plan to grow apples."

Do you see what I'm saying here, Mr. President?

dude ur losing me w this froot stuff

I guess what I'm saying is that we need to clean house.

Before our house is cleaned for us.

In the next election.

If I may clarify, sir . . .

i get it

chat with Wonderboy et al

there comes a time in each one of our lives . . .

I GET IT

yall want me 2 dump dick & rummy

dont like it

theyr my buds

cant bleev the base wants me 2 do it neithr

I agree the base might be angered.

Despite the veep's low ratings he's still popular with our most loyal supporters.

Key word here is "dump."

Now if either were to "resign" . . .

4get it

alredy ran it by dick

You already raised this with the vice president, sir?!

4 sur

i tell im evrything

hes my bvfl

I'm not familiar with that acronym, sir.

best veep 4 life

we wuz jus kickin bak

shootin squirrls off the truman balcony

way we do wen no1s lookin

(dont wrry karen—wuz jus a bb gun)

i sed sum ppl thot he shd go

we're all kinda wrried bout his helth

make way 4 08

yadda yadda

he wuz like no way

"promisd 2 serv so i'll serv"

"die w my boots on" etc

wat wuz i gna say??

man sumtimes i wish he wuznt such a tuff ass

bottom line: sum1 els is gna hav 2 break it 2 im

Who would you suggest, sir?

dunno!

dick dusnt lissen 2 any1 xept himself

That gives me an idea, Mr. President.

What if instead of asking him to resign

we put him in charge of a secret committee to find a new SecDef?

That way he'll review all the possible candidates

and then decide that the only person fit for the job is

dick cheney!

exactamundo

but wat bout rummy?

wher duz he go?

I think we make that the vice president's problem.

Karen's right, sir.

Secretary Rumsfeld DID just buy a lovely retirement place on the Eastern shore

just down the road from the veep's.

Excellent duck hunting country, sir.

If you see what I'm saying.

😮

😊

🙂

Mr. President! I in no way meant to imply . . .

u get 2 wrk on that nu *msg* karl

Right away sir.

chat with FlyChopper

6:10 p.m

yo bolty

headin 2 the mess?

texmex day!!

cd go 4 a chx tortilla

nada sour cream

guac on the side

xtra salsa

diet coke *no ice*

(nuff brain freezes round here!)

Auto-reply: Josh Bolten is away from his computer.

chat with BigBartlett

6:11 p.m.

danny boy!!

Yes, Mr. President?

u c boltass?

He's in his office, sir.

got his frikkin away msg

He's there, sir.

His door's open.

I can see his shoe.

I need im on IM

Perhaps he's on the phone.

PRONTO

Is there something I could help you with, sir?

neg

I'll go tell him.

"Be right back," Mr. President.

…

Mr. President?

wers boltass?

He is on the phone, sir.

did u tell im i need im PRONTO?

No, sir.

?!

😣

He waved me away.

He pointed to the phone and mouthed "Russert."

At least I think it was "Russert."

It could have been "Russians."

He's got a lot on his plate, sir.

o man

thissis sooo messd up

What is messed up, Mr. President?

this!!

im like THE. PREZ.

my plates full 2!

acshully its MT

thats the prob

i cant get boltass 2 do nuffin!!

I don't think you mean that, sir.

He's working flat-out around the clock for you.

Last night he was here until past midnight

and when I pulled in the lot at dawn
this morning

his motorcycle was already there.

yeh well hes got US wrkin flat out

don't like it

look @ the TIME!

It's just past six, sir.

xactamundo

wen hav u known me 2 b here past 6??

shd b upstairs

kickin bak

flippin on the game

but noo

im still @ my frikkin desk

tryin 2 make frikkin sens of his 5 pt "recvry plan"

It looks very promising, Mr. President.

i KNO recvry plans danno

theyr usually 10 steps

not "5 pts"

& they=1 thing

What's that, sir?

NO. FUN.

6:23 p.m.

Mr. President!

You're still in the office?

☺

hey harry

chattin w danno

l8r?

Of course, sir.

I was just following up on our "Italy" discussions.

no newz

workin on it

Thank you, Mr. President.

I know how much you care.

BTW, I'm headed down to the mess.

Can I bring you up anything?

no thanx harry

chat with HMiers

wuz hopin boltass wd do it

HMiers has gone offline.

chat with BigBartlett

6:25 p.m.

had 2 deal w harry

u c wat im sayin

i jus MENTION boltass & shes offline

we wer all so happy w andy

Andy Card was a fine chief of staff. But it was time for him to move on . . .

he knew how i likd evrything

lime w my bucklers

cheezbrgr med no pickls

this dude boltass

like he datd BO DEREK

i can tell u

no dude whos datd bo derek

gna b gettin me my cheezbrgr

tho mayb he'll get harriet off my case

I can understand why Harriet's emotional, sir.

This past week has been difficult for her.

I feel we've let her down again.

?

I'm doing everything within my power to track down the source of those unfavorable stories.

It saddens me that there could be someone in the executive branch who would, for lack of a better word, "trash" her behind her back.

It must be remembered—after all is said and done—she WAS our top choice for the Supreme Court.

im tryin 2 4get that

but watu mean *trash*?

Perhaps you didn't see the stories, Mr. President.

I certainly didn't put them on your desk.

They quoted "White House sources" as saying that Josh wanted to get rid of her because she was "incompetent."

Nasty stuff.

lol

Excuse me, sir?

chk ur sorces danno!

they wuz HARRY

she wuz leakin 2 the press!

I'm not following you, Mr. President.

HARRY. Wuz. The. Sorce.

I still don't understand, sir.

cant bleev i hav 2 spell this out

harry wantz 2 leave

like real bad

aftr the SCOTUS mess

we offrd her all kindza junk

rnc shit

cirkut judjships

but she dont like nun of it

shes like: aftr all my yrs of servis mr. president

id like sumpin a lttl bigr

sumpin mor FUN

so im like: wat

(cuz tween u & me danno this gurl knos nuffin bout partyin)

& shes like: italy

im like 😲

im thinkin: harry & my bud silvio?!?!

like how longs that bin goin on?

she cs my face

& she gets it

shes like omg

"not that sir!"

"i wuz talkin bout the embassy!"

Harriet Miers wants to be the U.S. Ambassador to Italy?

bingo

But, sir—correct me if I'm wrong—she doesn't speak Italian, does she?

duh

she knew crap bout constitutional law

but that didnt stop her from wantin SCOTUS

Mr. President, I share your admiration for Harriet in every way.

But I think at this point it will be difficult to give her the Italian embassy.

dbl duh

U try tellin harry that

meek ms miers

standin tween her & an appt she wants

is like standin tween bill clinton & a shrt rib

ive jus been puttin her off

tellin her 2 lay low

wait till the blood stops runnin thru the halls

wen boltasses raina terror is ovr

You know you're exaggerating, Mr. President.

We all welcome the change.

You made the right decision, sir.

Josh will have this place back on track in no time.

look!

hes evn got u suckin up!

& like hes not evn ONLINE

I'm just trying to persuade you that he's going to make things better for you, Mr. President.

For all of us.

And for the American people.

183

he sure aint makin things bttr 4 wonderboy

he blammd karl pretty gd

moved him from his big office 2 the broom closet cross the hall

It's been a very stressful time for all of us.

But I'm confident that now we can look forward to a more hopeful future.

One in which your legacy will be recognized and rewarded, in '06 and again in '08.

k but if u find me ded

bhind my desk

im NOT depressd k??

i hav NO suicidl tendencys

K??

Ha ha, Mr. President.

ditto 4 dick

Can we go back to something you said, sir?

make it quik

im gna eat my own arm

You didn't explain why Harriet leaked
bad press about herself.

Or maybe you did, but I still don't understand.

ez

boltass had the same reaction u did 2 italy

he's like no. way.

**so SHE leakd 2 the press that boltass
wuz dissin her**

made im look bad

a big bully

poor lttl ms miers

then he had 2 publikly take it bak

& he hadnt dunnit!!

shes not gna rest till he givs it 2 her

like i sed:

u don't mess w dirty harry

not evn boltass

she'll jus make his frikkin day

like she made rs

my bet: she gets italy

I'm sure you're right, sir.

On a separate note, I'm going to head down to the mess.

Can I get you something?

☺

The usual?

Extra salsa?

ur the mano danno

I just noticed Josh is off the phone.

Should I tell him to come see you?

nah

aint urjent no mor

dude!

"muy hombre"

1st day on the job!

u redy 2 kick ur 4mr amigos asses

prime time ??

you betcha sir!

start w colbear

ttl twerp

**didnt like the way he made funna me
@ the WH correspondents dinnr**

i wuz funnyr

WAY funnier, sir.

You outclassed him.

He'll be the first to learn that you don't
get far with this administration by
insulting the President.

make sur he lerns quik

I will, sir. And let me just say how much I appreciate this opportunity to work for you.

I'm honored to serve this adminstration.

& let me also say how glad I am that you've agreed to these one-on-one talks with me.

I'm confident we can relaunch this show

administration

to much higher ratings.

boltass shur aint gna do it

tells the press we gotta "get our mojo back"

like thats soo embarrassin

specially 2 r enemys!

osamas rofl

"his own dude sez hes lost his mojo!!"

like whos got it now

dr evil?!

nah I don't think McCain has it, sir.

188

anyway let's move on

these problems are no longer your problems

they're our problems

they're MY problems

& I'm going to solve them

u can hav em

seriously, I've been thinking hard

I've got some ideas

I'd like you to preview

roll em

let's start with the daily press briefing:

since we're redoing the whole briefing room
& press offices anyway

(BTW I can report, sir, that the people at
Fox were very happy with the new plans

they especially liked their wet bar & gym

& glass offices overlooking the rose garden

chat with Snoblowr

while David Gregory was heard muttering about his low ceilings

& the fact he'll not be able to push out from his desk

without hitting a wall!

heh heh

u c wer I put

boltass put

helen thomas?

no sir

tol her she wuz gna b bside the cabnet room

shes like THRILLD

4got 2 mention the wrd *filin*

as in *filin cabnet*

hilarious, Mr. President!

but lets not digress as we're about to go into a hard break

chow time!

yes

since we're remodelling the briefing room anyway . . .

u eatin in the mess 2day?

no sir

I was just going to grab a sandwich round the corner

eat at my desk

revise the architect's plans

depending on what you had to say about . . .

which sanwich joint?

Cosi

they make a wicked Italian meatball although the wasabi roast beef is good too.

sounds suspishus

suspicious?

that wer u blo-dried talkin heds get ur fancy grool?

like wats rong w the cafeteria

turkey lettus mayo

nuffin rong w that

wasabi

thats jus japaneez

4 ovrpricd

Cosi sells s'mores now too, sir

SMORES?

😛

I'll ask if they have them to go, sir.

YES

ok

we were just talking about the new briefing room . . .

o yeh

I'm very excited about this, Mr. President.

the old one is so 1960s: podium/rows of seats

too static

sets up a bad visual: "us against them"

if we're going to appeal to a younger hipper demographic

we need a younger hipper set

set?

briefing room

k

cuz ur in the wite house now

gotta think dignfied

hstrical

prez.i.den.shul.

sorry, sir.

old language dies hard.

w me all languaj dies hard

thats y i need u

& that's why we need to revisualize this room

I see: no podium

I see: tv monitors/windows/graphics

lots of ice blue/matte silver

the audience

press

seated in a circle

I stand in the middle with a cordless mike

no chair/no desk

active

engaged

think the old Phil Donahue meets Dr. Phil . . .

or Oprah meets Wolf Blitzer.

After a short grabby statement & the day's talking points

(which we can throw up as bullets on monitors O'Reilly-style)

I walk right into the audience

press

to take questions.

"David Gregory, what have you got to say?"

"What about answers on Iraq?"

"Okay, let's talk about that . . ."

fast-paced but friendly

"Helen, how do you react to what I just said?"

message: we're in control

it's OUR show.

it's no longer THEIR show.

in fact, we should think about renaming it:

"The White House Briefing with Tony Snow."

a few of my old sound buddies

have put together some theme music

uh tone?

I'm not quite done, sir

I want you to have the full picture

i.e. we can go to the monitors when we want to roll our own footage.

"take a look at some good news in Iraq"

"the stuff you guys aren't showing the folks at home"

how dya toast the marshmalos?

I don't follow you, sir.

4 the smores!

u need 2 toast the marshmalos

like thers no campfire in cosi rite?

they bring it to your table

a campfire?!

no it's more like a rustic disposable coleman

some sort of flammable goo in pottery

im not really sure

my kids get them

cuz I wuz thinkin we cd use the kichen here in the oval office

nvr use it xept 2 wash barneys feet

that would work, sir

but tell me

do you have any reaction to my pitch

plans

for the daily press briefing?

lemme scroll bak up

wuz thinkin bout smores

. . .

k jus red it

and . . . ?

dunno

cd wrk i ges

but wat bout wen thers bad newz?

i mean ALOTTA bad newz

like rite now

ur sayin we wd put up r own gd newz?

Not only that, sir

we could have our own "crawl"

?

the little band of type that runs across the bottom of the screen

ours would broadcast our take on the day's headlines

"higher oil prices good for Iraqi economy"

"President Bush announces new initiative to preserve dinner hour for families."

like that

but wat happns wen sumpin reel bad happns?

mayb we dont hav gd vishuls

in the event of that, sir, we'd go to b-roll

??

sorry

another industry term

stock footage of something happy or distracting

Cancun maybe

its an old fox news trick

whenever you have something really horrible

"homicide in paradise"

you roll footage of girls in bikinis shaking their boobs

put it on a loop

no one pays attention to the news reader
or the story

Fox has got a lot of that kind of b-roll

they've also got c-roll and dd-roll

cant say I like that 1 tone

I mean: I LIKE it

but it aint gna fly w the base

it aint prezidenshul

we could create our own b-roll, sir

something more appropriate

maybe the "Dallas Cowboys Cheerleaders"

bingo

if you like the concept I envision taking it beyond the daily briefing

to you & your events

u aint gettin me in a bikini

funny!

no I meant bringing the message "active & engaged" to everything you do

break the bubble!

like how?

look at illegal immigration

it's killing you in the polls

people hate it & you're seen as soft

we need to get you down to the border

think "COPS"

I see: cameras following the president
on a night raid

I see: the president shouting "Stop!
Freeze you [bleeping] coyote!"

I see: merciless thugs thrown to the ground

I see: the President holding them down
while border cops frisk the suspects

cut to the reveal: an 18-wheeler stuffed to
the gills with starving & thirsty mexicans

frightened moms

crying dirty babies

dads just trying to do the right thing

nice decent people who just want to work
hard in our country

cut to: the president helping them
out of the truck

passing out bottles of water, formula

grilling burgers on an open flame

ur remindin me of smores

sorry, sir

I'll get them right away

but what do you think of my "COPS:Presidential Edition"?

I wouldn't even ask for a credit on that one.

lemme think it ovr

run it by a few ppl

I understand, sir

get back to me whenever

FYI I'll be out of the office for the next couple of weeks.

takin a vacation alredy??!

not at all, Mr. President

I have a little time to kill before I officially take over

thought I'd send myself out on assignment

get some specials in the can

 have them ready to roll out with the new briefings

"Democracy in Afghanistan with Tony Snow"

"China: Friend or Foe? A Special Report by Tony Snow"

"Removing the Veil: The Secret Lives of Islamic Women"

the last one is part of our new series "Behind the Scenes with Tony Snow"

i got 1 4 u

how bout "the iraq war w tony snow"

mayb u wanna take credit 4 that?

l8r Mr. President . . .

Snoblowr has left the chat.

yo

karen?

u ther GF?

Certainly, sir.

How may I be of assistance?

need ur help

its dick

The vice president, sir?

uh huh

hes not bin rite 4 a long time

don't think i can send im out no mor

His health, sir? Is it worse?

nah

his healths gd

u kno the veep

hes like a timex

cd pull him bhind a speedboat

ovr a ramp

& thru a freakin flamin hoop

he'd keep on tickin

Then what, sir?

Elections are coming up.

We need him out there.

I KNO

bin 2 ashamd 2 tell any1

You and I share appropriate levels of trust, Mr. President.

I think you can tell me.

k

PLEEZ don't tell no 1

dicks bcom a . . .

. . .

. . .

A what, sir?

environut

I don't understand, Mr. President.

cmon

u kno

tree huggr

animl rites whacko

green green lima bean

the hol 9 yrds

GET IT?

The vice president has become an environmentalist?

thats the wrd I wuz lookin 4

Since when, sir?

I haven't noticed anything odd about him.

I DID notice that he was preferring the cottage cheese plate at the mess these days

but I thought it was just a diet thing.

startd bak wen he poppd that dude

The hunting accident?

yeh

he rlly freakd

stoppd huntin

@ 1st I thot he'd get ovr it

u kno

he's like sum nam vet

havin flashbax

then rummy is like WTF

dicks "anti-huntin"

sez he can hear them fat birds cryin "no" evrytime he razes his gun

That is a problem, sir.

I assume that means no more NRA fund-raisers.

duh

stoppd em rite away

And he was such a favorite.

wait

it gets wrse

so I send im up 2 canada

2 chek out the oil fieldz in albrta

im thinkin the site of it will do im gd

fill his hart w frikkin joy

ges wat???

I'm afraid to, sir.

he sez no way shd we dig up ther!!

he's wrried bout the "criticl ecorejuns"

im like: dick ther aint nuffin

NUFFIN

but blak flies

it looks like the effin moon!

but hes like: nooo

cant do it

cant go ther

now hes rantin bout gettin "biodeezl" from french fries

& puttin winmills on his ranch in wy

he LUUUVS the gore movie

"u gotta c it!!"

"plantry emergncy!"

"earths in troubl!"

he soundz like cpt kirk!

Does anyone else know about this, Mr. President?

I mean outside of his family?

In the administration?

rummys suspishus

karl knos but is 😶

thats it

we're fillin his sked w foto ops @ ol folks homes

cuz most of em r deaf

Good move, sir.

wat r we gna do???

we got 2 mor yrs!

& hes lobbyin 2 do a joynt presser w barbra

Your mother, sir?

streisand!

I think I know what to do, Mr. President.

It's bold. But it may work.

210

?????

Send him to Iraq, sir.

A two-year assignment to oversee
the cleanup of the country.

Lots for him to do: Chemical spills, hazmats,
standing sewage, restoring marshlands.

When he speaks of the "situation on the ground"

or the "devastated infrastructure"

no one will be the wiser.

Indeed, it will improve the image of
the whole administration.

You'll be seen as "walking the walk."

And I should add, there is excellent health and
emergency medical care in the front-line bases, sir.

Something to point out to Mrs. Cheney.

☺

Mr. President?

cd wrk . . .

CD WRK!

211

wait

Sir?

wat if he stages sum protest

like @ a refinry??

He'll be under the watch of the American military 24/7.

No chance of that happening, Mr. President.

gr8!

ur still the brainz round here

u kno that rite

I'll always be proud to serve you, sir.

9:17 a.m.

u awake yet?

wassup bro

man its erly 4 u

nvr 2 erly 4 golf

headin out 2 the ts

wer u @?

rite here

in the big wite crib

thats rite

u got the big par-tay 2nite

yeh

like *happy jul 4th*

aclu gna outlaw that 1 soon

discrmin8s agenst illgl amerikns

man i h8 this holiday

?!

gotta stay in this hot swamp

like who wants 2 b in dc on jul 4?

turistas from japan thats who

them & bigass donrs who wanna watch firewrks from my balcny

FUN

no kickin bak 4 kickass

uh uh

meet & greet

"cd u stand ovr here nxt 2 my wife mr prez wile I getta foto?"

cant get near the frikkin bbq

"ooo look @ that 1 ovr the monumnt!!"

"soooo amazin!"

man I seen it 5x alredy!!

wd rather b in TX

pullin brush & tyin sparklrs 2 barneys tail

feel 4 u bud

tho I kinda miss jul 4 @ the big wite crib

specially the "stand nxt 2 my wife" part

wher laura b @?

she sez hi 2 the gests

then vamooses up 2 the roof

2 smoke & hang w the twins

tuff

wher u b @?

man im in lttl rok

teachin hllry how 2 eat bbq

ur w hill?!

🫢

thats wrs than dc!

nah

its justa foto op

hill w the lttl folk @ lttl rok

(gotta rmind her 2 keep her pinkies in

wen shes chowin down on ribs)

aftr that she clears out bak 2 dc

"sry hon—duty calls"

my bud burkles pvt jet swoops in

& pix me up

"sry hon—booty calls!"

man u r so lucky

u gottit sooo gd rite now

u gotta hope she aint gettin it in 08

cuz ur life is OVR

i kno it

man im PRAYIN she aint gettin it

evn went 2 nashville ovr the wkend

2 patch it up w al bore

u hung w bore?!

uh huh

thats how desprat i am bud

suddnly hills polls r goin thru the roof

aint no 1 can match her now

(thanx 2 that ol clinton majik ahem)

& shes stoppd takin my advis

its bad

ur advis?

dude U knew that wuz bad

but SHE didnt kno it wuz bad

im like "hon stay strong on the war"

"stand up 4 ur principls"

"b the politician i nvr wuz"

"ignor the far left baby"

"u gotta get bhind lieberman"

that shit

she wdnt lissen?

not wen I told her 2 bak lieberman

man I nearly had her!

that wda sunk her!

"hillary throws fund-raiser for lieberman"

bam—ded!

but she lookd @ me all suspishus

like she found sum blak thong in my sok drawr

she found a blak thong in ur sok drawr???

META4 ALRT!

I sed *like*

o

wait

u ment similee alrt

?

wen u use like or as

fyi

datsa similee

sins wen r U the gramma king?

dude I LIV w a school teachr

k

ANYHOO

i think shes on2 me

el draggo

ttlly!

watr we

u

gna do bout it?!

i tol u!

 i bit the bullet

hauld my ass down 2 nashville

& made nice 2 bore

whoa

thats tuff

had 2 b dun

y?

cuz hes my only hope man!

who els hav i got??

hes ona roll w this book/movie crap

he cd do it!

& im not the only 1 who thinks so

(calls hisself in privat btw "comebak kid—the sequel")

(like: BARF)

(& i don mean that as a similee)

tell me bout it

get this:

so i pull up @ his big nu crib

(& man its BIG—googles bin gd 2 that boy)

im thinkin: in/out

slap on the bak

yak bout ol times

pitch him sum advis

then im on my way 2 lttl rok 4 t-off time

no way ur outta there in undr 4 hrs

make it: 18 HRS!!

missd my frikkin plane!

o man

how cd I 4get?!!

wat happnd?

bore opens the door hisself

gets that look he gets

the icecap melts . . .

"bro!" he sez

he bearhugs me 4 like 5 mins

i cant BREETH

finally im like gaspin "bro I gotta use ur hed"

so he like shows me 2 the hed

& comes in w me!!!!!

no way

way

222

cuz u cant jus take a whizz @ bores house w/out a freakin lecshur

"don't let looks deceev u billy boy its all septic"

"heres the biodegradabl papr—don't use 2 much or itll clog the system"

dude im wettin myself!

yeh well i wuz wettin myself

"ok bro thanx uh gotta go REAL BAD"

but it wuz like that the whole time

he had a DAYLONG PROGRAM

he calld it "a program of reconciliation"

hes gotta sho me EVRYthing

think "MTV cribs" meets "National Geographic"

gotta inspect the "smart rm" in the basement

ooh & aw ovr his solar panels & compostr

finally wen im like DYIN he leads me in2 this huge screenin rm

im thinkin uh oh i kno wats comin

he sez: lemme sho u wat ive bin up 2

o no

not the moovie!!

WRSE

the UNCUT version!

😮

"this 1 has a lot mor prsnl stuff innit"

darn rite

its 4 HRS long!

family vacations

karennas kids

like sum hellish xmas card ona loop!

i havent evn had a glass o watr

& im like scrd 2 ask

u kno in case I get the "watr lecshur"

man u wanna subject sum terrorst prisners 2 legl torture

jus lok em in a screenin rm w bore!!!

howdu escape?!

I DIDN'T

aftr the movie he wantd 2 play touch ftball . . .

then tippr wantd me 2 look @ her fotos . . .

(memo 2 god: no more grandkids 4 that woman!)

by that pt id missd the plane

theyr like: gr8! u can stay w us! we'll have bbq! its solr powrd!

so then bore & i stay up 2 play hearts

"jus like ol times" he keeps sayin

im fnlly makin sum hedway . . .

ur winnin?

no!

on my mishun!

i start givin him sum advis

srsly GD advis

like the kinda advis ppl pay me $$$$$$

ive got his whole winnin campaign laid out on the table

like sum delishus gourmet buffet

all hes gotta do is fill his frikkin plate

suddnly hes like no no no

"lets not spoil the moment w politics"

inside im goin arrrrghhh!

so watu do?

so I went 2 bed

lay awake till it wuz dawn

then boltd b4 he cd ply me w tipprs "homemade bran muffns"

is he gna lissen 2 u?

he duznt lissen 2 any1

dudes hopeless

ttlly hopeless

hes gna blo it this time 2

shda remembrd

i gess id just blockd it

like sum bad memry from nam

u didn't go 2 nam

o rite

hey neither did u

mayb we've both blockd it

gd line

but it wont fly in 08

gna hit the linx now

no cheatin!

ha ha

chat with Ladeezman42

happy 4th

u 2 bud

Ladeezman42 has left the chat.

chat with BigBartlett

9:03 a.m.

I've just received confirmation, Mr. President.

The Pope is now online.

he aint showin up

Give it a moment sir.

He doesn't just "pop up" like others.

His Holiness "materializes."

kewl—ther he is!

but his *away* msg is still on

Give it another moment, sir.

now it sez *receptive*

That's the go-ahead, sir.

Are you sure you don't want me or
Condi to join the chat?

nope

keep it pvt

mano a mano

Okay, Mr. President.

Just don't start "confessing."

Ha ha

I mean: Ha ha, sir.

9:08 a.m.

ur holiness?

Auto-Reply: This message is intended for the recipient shown. It contains information that is confidential and protected from disclosure. Any review, dissemination, or use of this transmission or its contents by persons or unauthorized employees of the intended organizations is strictly prohibited. The contents of this message do not necessarily represent the views or policies of the Catholic Church, the Vatican, or any of its pastoral representatives or followers worldwide.

Forgive the disclaimer, brother. The Vatican insists that it now accompany all my remarks, written and spoken, private and public.

They say it is only temporary, until we are able to put in place a panel of linguistic and religious experts to assess and approve in advance any official statements relating to Islam.

However, I fear that, like so many impermanent measures, adopted in times of crisis, it may prove to be permanent.

Then the great dialogue between Christianity and Islam of which I dream will never take place, as our side shall be effectively silenced by the dictatorship of violence.

Woe for all of humanity should that come to pass.

But forgive me for burdening you with my own troubles.

What is it that you wished to speak with me about?

: - * -O-

Although I try to incorporate science with faith—insisting, as I do, that a mastery of modern technology should not prevent or diminish belief in God—for the life of me I do not understand this symbol you just used.

im kissin ur ring

Ah!

so ur holiness . . .

i jus wantd 2 xpress my supprt

ur undr alotta fire rite now

(4giv the metafor)

kno how it feels benny

dept of bin ther dun that

but u cant bak down

gotta push bak

if u dont mind me sayin

ur a tuffass

like that in a pope

jus like the last dude

j2p2

he wuz a tuffass

U may b evn tuffer

Thank you, brother.

232

Without courage we should have no conviction. And without conviction we should have no courage.

exactamundo

no need 2 say sry

Yes: We can apologize for our actions but not for the truth.

We can apologize for unexpected consequences to our words, but not for those who misunderstand our words and use them as an excuse to commit violence.

EXACTAMUNDO

I deeply regret what my words have wrought.

And yet, what sort of religious person defends the peace of his faith . . . by shooting a nun?

What sort of religious person replies to the accusation that his faith is spread by the sword . . . by threatening death by the sword?

is this a trik question?

how bout: islamonuts for $500 jack

Let us not single out faiths, brother. Let us use the rhetorical question to look within ourselves, and even at our own histories.

im witu pope

like they accuse me of messin up in iraq

but hell

heck

if u guys had handld the crusades proprly

we cdve solvd this problemo 1000 yrs ago

(no offens!)

No offense taken, brother.

That was what I was trying to allude to in my speech.

The question is: Are God's teachings open to interpretation? Can we apply our own moral view to His actions? Is the violence we encounter in the Bible a metaphor—or something we must take as a literal call to slaughter?

I think few will dispute that Catholic thought and debate has moved forward since the Crusades.

tho ur alwys being 2nd gessed by pundits

That is true.

& now ur own peeps r risin up agenst u

those librl priests!

theyr like: waa! we didn't sign up 4 this!

we didn't sign up 2 get shot at!

tell em 2 stop criticizn u

tell em its uncatholic

tell em theyr only givin aid & comfort 2 the enemy

You mean to the Muslims?

no

the protestnts

I shall consider your advice.

well dont 4get

im witu

got ur bak

& like if u need xtra security . . .

I am secure in the knowledge that God will protect me.

But thank you.

u can alwys call on my bud silvio

he may b outta powr

but hes still got frends

kno wat im sayin?

The former prime minister has been greatly supportive, yes.

lemme try agen:

HES. GOT. FRIENDS.

nice lttl mosk u got here

they cd take care of it 4 u

& silvio . . .

he's no choirboy but still a vry gd catholic

lot of sins 2 atone 4

sure he'd b DLITED 2 help

chat with Ben16

now u kno wat im sayin ur holiness?

Yes.

God's ways are mysterious.

Indeed.

Ben16 has recessed from the chat.

chat with Ladeezman42

8:09 p.m.

dude!

Auto-reply: The Clinton Global Initiative is designed to inspire action. Find out how you can contribute by going to **www.clintonglobalinitiative.org**.

aw man

kno ur ther

ur watchin americas nxt top model

cmon

dont try 2 duck me

Auto-reply: The Clinton Global Initiative is designed to inspire action. Find out how you can contribute by going to **www.clintonglobalinitiative.org**.

k fine

b that way

u may b *away* but ur not *offline*

i kno u can c this

so i'll jus say wat im gna say

Auto-reply: The Clinton Global Initiative is designed to inspire action. Find out how you can contribute by going to **www.clintonglobalinitiative.org**.

thot we had a dealio

"I don't blame u 4 osama"

"u don't blame me 4 osama"

that chris wallace intervu wuznt cool

repeat: NOT. COOL.

Auto-reply: The Clinton Global Initiative is designed to inspire action. Find out how you can contribute by going to **www.clintonglobalinitiative.org**.

like wat wuz that bout???

u lookd crazy

way loco

all that rite wing conspircy crap

blamin me/blamin fox news etc

u KNO u sat on ur ass 4 8 yrs

8 YRS!

lettin osama blo up *watevah*

"how bout sum uss cole w ur khobar twrs?"

"mayb ud like the world trade centr as a side . . . ?"

"the whole things goin on special on 9/11"

then like now ur *away*

inspirin acshun

yeh rite

key wrd: *inspirin*

sur aint *doin*

k

sed wat i needd 2 say

sum bud u r

gna turn on the ball game

hold it rite ther!!

SIT

NOW

knu it!

knu u wer online!

u did dick bout osama b4 9/11!

u cda stoppd 9/11 if ud cared more bout securty

than pullin brush in tx!

geez man it wuz a nu term

i nvr do well my 1st yr

im still tryin 2 figr out wher my frikkin classes r!

well dont go givin me this "dealio" crap

we didnt hav no deal

DID

chkd w poppy

he remembrs

few mos aftr 9/11

he sed "this aint a moment 4 u boys 2 get in2 the blame game"

remembr?

that time we were all playin horseshoos @ camp dave?

(i beat jeb)

u sed "ur rite mr b"

"aint no gd pointin fingrs"

"this is biggr than all of us"

so wat wuz all that fingr pointin w wallace????

lttl creep

jus wantd 2 punch him!

wipe that smug lttl smile offa his face

felt GD

makin that twerp squirm

sho im we clintons dont hafta take that shit

havent felt that good ina long time

not sins i dissd jennings

well u mighta felt gd but I sur didnt appreshiate it

& its not like u did urself any gd

like here u r

mr statesman

mr globl inishutiv

shakin hands w gates & buffett

lettin the press kiss ur ass

"oo he shd b the nxt sec-gen of the UN!"

& u go on sum paranoid rant!

hed slap dude!

man u jus uppd the clinton street cred w the lefty whackos!

ur a star on utube—u & george allen!

u may b rite

jus felt so dam gd

yeh well thats alwys ur xcuse

aint gna help u sink hllry

if that wuz ur plan

(which i thot it wuz)

not like u guys r helpin me out here

hllry looks hot compard 2 dat boob allen

& he wuz like ur front runner!

that must b a 1st!

wat?

a jew runnin 4 prez?

no!

that the stupidst guy in the race wuz jewish

as monica wd say: wat a shonda

?

an embarrsmnt!

4 the jews!

cmon

its not like ur surpriz jews r any bttr

u guys had albright

albright jewish!

muy shockr!

she wuznt all jewish

wuznt all brite neither

& look @ kerry!

**man no 1 cared that he acceptd
"irishman of the yr" award . . .**

like 4 X in a row!

& hes as jewish as allen

didnt c that come up in the debates

thats cuz he wasnt such a schmuck

stop w the hebru

aint gettin it

yiddish

look it up

www.yiddishdictionaryonline.com

ull c ur foto ther

comes aftr putz

lol

NOT

dude i thot we cdnt hand u a lamer candidat than hillry!

get this:

wuz @ a funraisr 4 hill

sry *fundraisr*

(cuz they sur AINT fun)

peeps r xcited

u kno: hill! hill! hill!

she walks in & waves

peeps clappin & whistlin

then she opens her big piehole

man!

its like she lets off vrbl sarin!

folks grabbin ther throats . . .

passin out . . .

like nooo pls stop!

rofl

u evr notis how she moovs her hed
wen she talks?

uh no

side 2 side like an automatic sprinklr:

chook chook chook chook chook—
change direction!

blatatatatatata—change direction!

omg if she gets electd

4 yrs of soakin the ppl

& 4 DRI yrs 4 me

yeh well u guys cd nomin8 brttny speers & clean up

im lowr in the pollz than HER

& that chick nrly dropped her frikkin baby!

well u dudes keep throwin up shmegeges like allen

& brittny speers will be ur candidat 4 08!

I SED: cut w the hebru

YIDDISH

search wrd: buffoon

o wait—here's u:

noyef

heres a cloo: its wat hillry wd call u

knok it off

jus admit it: we fieldd bttr jews than u

rubin, reich, emanuel

we have the neocons

GREENSPAN

josh boltens a jew

JOHN bolton acts jewish

larry summers

lieberman!

wait

duz he count on r side or urs?

u can have him

k

still

u havent xplaind y u blew up @ wallace

went all *meshugeh*

dunno bud

felt like ol times I ges . . .

& I did owe hllry sumthin

?

chek out **this foto** goin round the internet

thats me w my arm round the hot chik in front

not bad 4 the prez of iowas young democrats!

sum shainkeit

wat bristen!

ur catchin on dude

unfortunatly so wuz hillry

a bump in her polls

will distract her from the bump in my pants

kno wat im sayin

got it bud

chat with Ladeezman42

ur still a pisk-malocheh

shalom dude

Ladeezman42 has left the chat.

chat with BigBartlett

7:05 a.m.

danno!

u ther???

WHER R U????

wtf

UR SUPOSD 2 B THER!

Here, Mr. President.

I was getting a coffee from the mess.

Jogged to my desk when I heard your pinging.

Sorry to keep you waiting, sir.

dude this foley shits bad

BAD

. . .

r u like THER????????

im *waitin*

Yes, it's bad, sir.

And yes I'm here.

I was typing with one hand.

Wiping coffee off my pants with the other.

o gr8

like ur touchin ur pants wile we're IMing?

is like evry1 in this town a SICKO?

"Mopping" might be a better verb, sir.

In any case, the burning sensation has almost stopped.

k so wen ur finishd cleanin urself weve a big problem here scotty

MAJR problemo

We've been working on little else, Mr. President.

Rove, Bolten, Snow, & I will have a comprehensive strategy worked out by the 9 a.m. meeting

essentially expanding upon your initial statement of earlier this week.

Karl has some charts and preliminary data on possible electoral repercussions

Tony will present his five-prong communication "blitzkrieg" as he calls it

yeh yeh yeh

save it 4 the meetin

im not talkin bout THAT

Excuse me, sir?

We're talking about the Foley fallout, right?

DUH

Sorry, but I'm confused, Mr. President.

Which aspect of it am I not addressing?

duznt any1 els round here think xept me?

dude look wat we're doin RITE NOW

We're discussing what we're going to do about Foley?

no

we're IMin

instant messagin

Of course, sir.

I thought that was obvious.

o man

(slap 4hed)

danno how many x a day do we IM?

I'd say on average maybe 6 or 8 times a day.

More when the World Series is going on.

Then we might go as many as 10 times per day.

gd

now lemme ask u this:

did it evr occur 2 u b4 foley . . .

that IMs cd b SAVED?

Oh.

To be honest, sir . . .

no.

dude we're talkin a gazillion chats

Yes.

wrld leders

condi/karl/karen/U

I understand.

the frikkin POPE!

"Got it," Mr. President.

man I cant SLEEP thinkin bout wats out ther

10-4

not like im sum prevert

dont talk dirty 2 teenagers

MUY COMPRENDE EL PRESIDENTE

I'm on it, sir.

I'll find out.

o man

What, sir?

I mean, don't tell me

online.

teenagers!

the twinz

lord knos wat they IM

I'll report back ASAP, Mr. President.

in person

face to face

Let me add that it would be prudent to end this conversation

and avoid all future conversations

until such time as we have further information

concerning our online security.

BigBartlett has left the chat.

1:48 p.m.

dude!

whaddya find out?!

CT

they saved or wat???

CANT TALK

im dyin

wat r we gna do?!

WILL. LET. U. KNO.

l8r

K?!

cuz if thers any chans

ANY

we gotta shut this thing down NOW

go on offens

lemme fone u

u cant

im ona plane

how can u IM?!

qatar air 1st class

wireless internet/no fone

go figur

weird frikkin islamos

correction:

While traditional in their beliefs, the peace-loving Muslims of Qatar embrace all the comforts and conveniences of the 21st century.

watr u talkin bout??

copied it off the inflite zine

gtta watch wat we say

NO KIDDIN

wich is y im sayin NADA

cmon bud

gimme a hint

r u lookin in2 "it"

+

gd

1 mor

no!

pls

i'll b careful!

us christians can b *saved*

hav u bin *saved*?

cd w b *saved* 2gether?

r u on ambien?

cuz ur makin no sense

u kno I luv jesus

wuz savd a long time ago

thats how I got here

God savd me so I cd save amerka

dam

thats not wat im askin

lemme try agen:

wen u pull brush @ crawford

do u *save* it?

Like r ther gr8 big files

piles

of brush sittin round

4 any1 2 find

or dya get ridda it RITE AWAY

kno wat im sayin?

😊

chat with Ladeezman42

dont play dum

u kno wat im gettin @

K

i'll say this:

(& don't ask 4 mor cuz we shdnt b DOIN THIS)

theyr lookin rite now 2 c if the *brush is cleard*

cuz I nvr sav brush

NVR

useless stuff

fire hazrd

but sum ppl mite

u kno

who dont kno bttr

dude u wdnt BLEEV wat sum folks save

(e.g. staind dresses)

rite

lemme kno asap

cuz we may hafta go in & rlly pull out that brush

pull it real hard

cuz thats the only way 2 do it

pull hard till thers nuffin left

uh dude?

u mite wanna refrase that last bit

sounds like foley

gross

k 4get that part

but u got the msg?

yes

g2g

Kickass43 has left the chat.

3:27 p.m.

Mr. President?

u got the 411?

Yes, sir.

May I come in and see you?

cant

got sum skoolkids waitin

bottomline it 4 me quik

I'd rather not do so online, sir.

uh oh

Well—it may not be that bad, Mr. President.

I can explain it all when the children leave.

tell me like *in jenral*

b quik

Okay.

In general, there's good news and bad news, sir.

The good news is that while traditionally it's White House policy to save every scrap of paper of every administration—

including personal notes, e-mails, Post-its, and even those doodles of Barney you do when you're bored—

there had been no policy concerning instant messaging.

The technology was simply too new when we arrived in 2000.

thats gd!

The bad news is that Harriet Miers . . .

o no

when she served as staff secretary . . .

o man

took it upon herself to correct this omission.

Working with our geek squad, she managed to implement an auto-save feature on every White House computer . . .

evn IMs?!

Yes, sir.

As she put it, "History will be safe."

I mean *saved*

u bttr get in here

f2f

Right away, sir.

chat with Ugogrl

9:17 p.m.

Mr. President?

It's Madam Speaker.

Still hard to get used to, isn't it?

I mean the "madam" part!

☺

Auto-reply: The President of the United States welcomes your input. Please direct correspondence to the White House, 1600 Pennsylvania Avenue NW, Washington, DC 20500. Or send your comments to <u>comments@whitehouse.gov</u>. Due to the large volume of e-mail received, the White House cannot respond to every message.

A *little bird* tells me you're a big IM user

hint: it's NOT Harriet Miers

(who I think is fabulous btw

maybe not Supreme Court material

—we have others for that!—

but certainly a groundbreaker for women)

I'm sorry you chose to dump her in such an unceremonious way.

Auto-reply: The President of the United States welcomes your input. Please direct correspondence to the White House, 1600 Pennsylvania Avenue NW, Washington, DC 20500. Or send your comments to comments@whitehouse.gov. Due to the large volume of e-mail received, the White House cannot respond to every message.

Okay, it WAS Harriet

who fyi doesn't blame YOU for dumping her.

she blames Josh Bolten

I'd say she's still bitter

we had coffee in the cafeteria today

she's looking for work

says she might even consider coming over to the Democrats

so you might want to switch off your *away* message

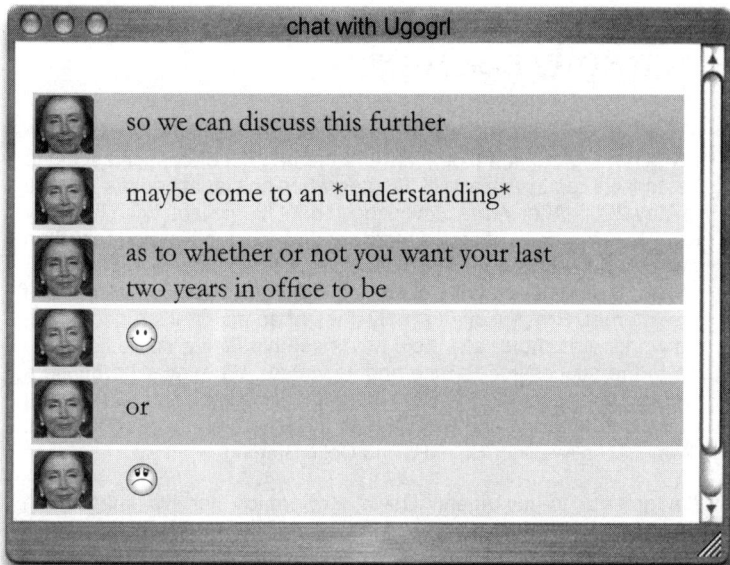

chat with Ugogrl

so we can discuss this further

maybe come to an *understanding*

as to whether or not you want your last two years in office to be

☺

or

☹

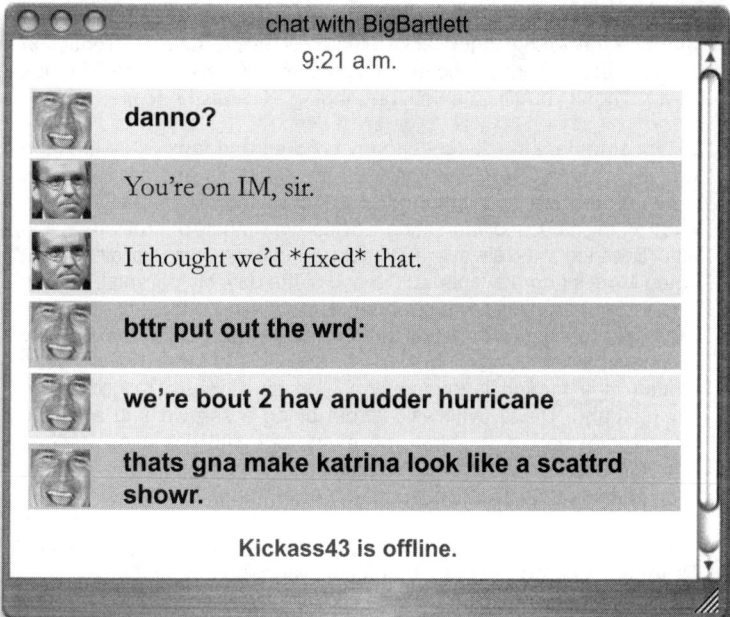

chat with BigBartlett

9:21 a.m.

danno?

You're on IM, sir.

I thought we'd *fixed* that.

bttr put out the wrd:

we're bout 2 hav anudder hurricane

thats gna make katrina look like a scattrd showr.

Kickass43 is offline.

ACKNOWLEDGMENTS

The President's Secret IMs began as a feature on the *Huffington Post*. I was among the first bloggers (and the handful of conservatives) to be conscripted by Arianna Huffington when she launched the website in May 2005. After years of working in print journalism, I can honestly say I've rarely been offered a more creative—or fun—opportunity than I've had with Arianna at HuffPo. Arianna is charismatic and generous, always urging her contributors to explore the limitless possibilities of the Internet. Roy Sekoff is simply a joy of an editor; it's a good thing he works at home or else he'd never see his family, so dedicated is he to the success of the site and its writers. Whenever I propose a wacky idea—such as the IMs—his reply, unfailingly, is, "Go for it." I thank both Arianna and Roy, and all the others on the HuffPo team: Romi Lassally, Elinor Shields, and Colin Sterling.

I'm grateful to my agent, David McCormick, for his imagination and vision: He believed that the IMs could work as a book when I had doubts. Patrick Price at Simon Spotlight Entertainment was a pleasure to work with—despite his annoying habit of being proven right whenever the two of us disagreed. Mitzi Hamilton created the ingenious template for the chats. The design was brilliantly carried out by Jane Archer and Becky Munich, with the help of production editor Brenna Sinnott. Michael Nagin is responsible for the hilarious cover. Thank you all so much for bringing "Kickass43" to life.

My most fervent thanks goes to my children and family: My teenage daughter Miranda inspired the idea for the chats and proved to be a superb teacher and editor of IM slang; my son Nathaniel's gimlet-eyed publishing and marketing advice was much appreciated; and little Beatrice was always a reliable source of comedic distraction when Mom's humor waned at the end of the day. My parents, Yvonne and Peter Worthington, have been encouraging recipients of every creative project I've thrust at them since I was a child, their loyalty extending even to reading the IMs, despite the latter having been written in a foreign language (lol). And as always, I'm grateful to my husband, David, who aside from being a shrewd and amusing observer of politics, inspires me every day with his love, wisdom, courage, honesty, and good humor. Few things make me happier than hearing his distinctive laugh echoing through our home.

Oh yes—and thanks to the entire Bush administration, especially President George W. Bush. Who could've made this stuff up?

ABOUT THE AUTHOR

DANIELLE CRITTENDEN is the author of the bestselling *Amanda Bright @ Home*, the first novel ever to be serialized by the *Wall Street Journal*. She is also the author of the nonfiction book *What Our Mothers Didn't Tell Us: Why Happiness Eludes the Modern Woman*.

Crittenden blogs regularly for the *Huffington Post*. Her articles and essays have appeared in the *Wall Street Journal*, the *New York Times*, the *Washington Post*, the *Weekly Standard*, *National Review*, *Ladies' Home Journal*, *Redbook*, *Reader's Digest*, and other publications. She has appeared on NBC's *Today* show, ABC's *20/20* and *Nightline*, and network news shows, as well as numerous programs for CSPAN, MSNBC, PBS, CNN, Fox, and CBC. She is also a regular guest on talk-radio programs across the country, and is an occasional contributor to National Public Radio.

Born in Toronto, Canada, Crittenden is married to journalist and bestselling author David Frum, a former special assistant and speechwriter to President George W. Bush. They have three children and live in Washington, D.C.